A Nuclear Family:

Coming of Age in Oppenheimer's Secret City

Ellen Wilder Bradbury-Reid

E. Marshall Wilder

The authors have used their best efforts to verify all names, dates and events portrayed in this book. However, no representation or warrantees are made or implied as to their accuracy. The authors do not warrant the performance, effectiveness or applicability of any of the listed or links in the e-book. All links are for information purposes only and are not warranted for content, accuracy or any other implied or explicit purpose. We have also included other first-person accounts of what it was like to be inside Los Alamos during the Manhattan Project.

This book is dedicated to our parents, Dulcenia Straeffer Wilder and Edward Wilder.

Table of Contents

Introduction
Growing up at Los Alamos: A Personal History of the Manhattan Project

We cannot undo what was done. No matter how many
times we re-examine it, the fact remains: the genie does not
go back into the bottle. It hovers above us.
(Ellen Bradbury-Reid)

Many books and documentaries have been written about
the Manhattan Project—the infamous endeavor that
developed the atomic bomb during World War II in Los
Alamos, New Mexico. You can find biographies of its first
director, J. Robert Oppenheimer and a few lively books
about the early days written by scientists' wives. And there
are books about the scientists' children with charming
interviews and stories. It was a utopian setting where men
cooked up weapons that continue to haunt us today and
where their families lived unusual lives in a town created
for this singular purpose.

My brother, Marshall Wilder, and I have written this
account about what it was like to live inside a secret town
dedicated to making the most destructive weapon ever

conceived. Although a child's point of view is not going to untangle the complicated web of what happened in Los Alamos, Marshall and I want to add our bit: memories of growing up in an unusual place and time. Looking back at our lives gives a glimpse about how things were inside that "hinge" of time. Even as small children we knew that whatever they were doing was a big deal. Somehow, we knew that. Nobody told us. We just knew.

And it was. And we are still coming to terms with it.

This book is a collection of my memories and some of the stories that I heard about the project. Marshall, who is three years younger than me, has embellished some of my stories and added others. They seem worth telling after all these years because the Manhattan Project has taken on a semi-mythic status. These are personal stories that may help humanize those times when the United States undertook a necessary and terrifying project.

Because everything at Los Alamos was secret, it took the families of those scientists and engineers years to learn what they had been doing. We never asked anybody what their father did.

Our family moved to Los Alamos in the spring of 1945 when Marshall and I were little kids. Scientists had determined that the method they had devised to detonate the plutonium for one of the bomb designs would fizzle or pre-detonate. Our father—Daddy—was sent to Los Alamos to help solve this problem. He and his team had to figure out a new way to make plutonium detonate.

Most of the time Daddy blew things up. At one point during the spring of 1945 his team was detonating more than 26 tons of high explosives a month - almost a ton a day every month. They were testing various configurations of shaped explosive lenses intended to surround the plutonium in the bomb known as Fat Man—the one used in the Trinity test and the Nagasaki drop. The technology they developed back then is still how most nuclear weapons are made. Strict secrecy was intended to prevent this information from getting out so that the Nazis, and later the Soviets, couldn't make a bomb. But of course, they did. We have also provided a view of S-Site written by our father about his own workplace. It remains the only account of what went on inside the most secret part of the secret city.

***

When I was six, I got my first security clearance at Los Alamos. At the time, my ambition was to be a spy. I thought I had figured out the secret, all by myself, of what was going on around me. After all, if whatever they were doing was so dangerous that even little children could not be trusted, then it must be really interesting.

I was just old enough to be aware of a larger world where something important was happening. I understood that it was very dangerous. Because of that, we had to move from our home in Louisville, Kentucky to a white canvas tent in remote northern New Mexico. Once there, Daddy told me he was working on a new kind of bomb, something, he said, that had never been done before. That sounded exciting. I wanted to know what it might be. I even thought I might help.

Looking back on growing up in Los Alamos in the 1940s and 50s, we felt a bit like zebras: the people in surrounding communities viewed us as slightly different.

The local Indian pueblo people in northern New Mexico say they live in a "center space," which is safe, and when you go out of that special space to the "outside" world you have to be a little more careful. We, too, lived in a special space. It was defined by tall fences topped by concertina wire guarded by military police who patrolled the fence in jeeps.

We had fences and passes and guards, good schools, and even, eventually, grass (though hardly anybody in Santa Fe had lawns in those days). But we knew that we should be a bit wary of talking too much or winning too many football games or the state debating contest. Being special isn't always comfortable.

We lived in a synthetic town that was a cross between an Army base and an American suburb. Los Alamos had been an elite boy's school, but in 1942 the Army bulldozed most of that and built a laboratory with buildings made of asbestos shingle siding surrounding a pond with a few ducks and rows of prefabricated houses strung out on the flat mesa top.

The population of Los Alamos was thrown together with a sense of urgency driven by the desire to end the war. The population of the town was young with an average age of 26. J. Robert Oppenheimer, a respected scientific leader, operated in some ways like a military dictator. And there was General Groves, who *was* a military dictator. And there were the rest of us. This is our story.

Chapter 1
Daddy

In 1944, our father, Edward Wilder, was a chemical engineer. He grew up in Louisville, Kentucky, and earned a Bachelor of Science degree in chemical engineering from the University of Louisville Speed School. His father, our grandfather didn't work since his family had left him a considerable estate. He had a large house and led the good Southern life even though his family had lost a significant sum of money when one of their banks closed during the Great Depression.

Edward Wilder, circa 1943

After graduation, Daddy took a job as the chemist at a local microbrewery in Louisville. He had tried to enlist in the military right after Pearl Harbor but was rejected because he had spots on his lungs, probably remnants of the rheumatic fever he had as a child. He joked that his work at the brewery, making beer was his important contribution to the war effort.

But the war grew in scope, he was told to report again for a physical. This time his lungs were fine, so in 1944 he joined the Navy.

Daddy's "contribution to the war effort"

He told us that after basic training, the other recruits were shipped out to join the fleet but he was told to remain in the barracks. It turned out that the Navy had discovered he had a technical degree. This made him "officer material" so he was sent to Officer Candidate School (OCS).

After a few weeks, before he finished OCS, the Navy sent him to Oak Ridge, Tennessee to use his chemical training on a secret project. He was tapped to help figure out how to separate uranium 235, a fissile isotope that can sustain a nuclear chain reaction from the predominate isotope uranium 238. The scientists were working feverously to make an atomic bomb.

Chapter 2
Leadership at Los Alamos

Our story revolves around a group of men developing and building the world's first atomic bombs in a remote location. Although Los Alamos was a small secret military installation, the men chosen to work there were allowed to bring their families. Theoretically, this would make them happier or less stressed and cause them to work harder . . . and maybe it did.

These hand selected, brilliant scientists and engineers, drawn from the top universities in America and free Europe, had access to every resource the United States could offer. They honestly didn't know if this sort of weapon could be developed. They believed that they were in a race against Nazi Germany. But they did not know if it was possible to win.

The military boss of Los Alamos was General Leslie Richard Groves, Jr. In 1942, he made the unlikely choice of J. Robert Oppenheimer to be the scientific director of the Manhattan Project. Oppenheimer, who was 38 years old and was teaching at Berkeley and Cal Tech, had done some important work in physics but had not received a Nobel Prize which would have given him better prestige for recruiting the world's best physicists. He smoked constantly, either cigarettes or a pipe, loved spicy food, and made and drank very strong martinis. Later on, it was rumored that he had placed a case of vermouth at ground zero of the Trinity Fat Man bomb test and from that time forward the way to make the perfect martini was to fill a glass with very cold gin and hold it out the window for a minute so the right amount of vermouth would fall(out) into it. He had a kind of opacity and a fastidious intellectualism that often left him completely blind to the political realities facing him. But he had great assets; he understood the importance of gesture and style and had an "aura" about him. He felt he was exempt from the rules and mores of conventional behavior.

Top: This cocktail napkin is from a bar in Santa Fe from a period after the war. The story of Oppenheimer's recipe for the perfect martini had gotten out, so this pays homage to the martini and radioactivity. The art mimics the International Radiation Symbol first used in 1946 at the University of California Berkeley Radiation Laboratory (Bottom).

The power of Oppenheimer's personality and quick mind made some other important physicists nervous. When the ordinarily loquacious Edward Teller first met Oppenheimer, he remembers he was so impressed he could not speak, hardly typical for Teller. As director of Los Alamos, Oppenheimer had to use all his abilities because he was, in Groves' words, "in charge of a bunch of prima donnas."

While Los Alamos was the creation of Oppenheimer and Groves, the atmosphere was Oppenheimer's. Even Teller, who eventually became bitter and jealous of Oppenheimer, agreed that Oppenheimer was the only man who could have pulled off the project.

Oppenheimer was familiar with the mountains of Northern New Mexico. He and his younger brother, Frank, owned a small cabin in a remote part of a high mountainous region known as the Pecos wilderness. Oppenheimer had fallen in love with that cabin which he named Perro Caliente, or "Hot Dog" the moment he saw it. It gave him a sense of psychic balance. The cabin has a magnificent view of the surrounding mountains where Aspen trees grow to the edge of meadows and were covered with fields of blue wild iris in the spring. The cabin is beautifully crafted, built by a German or Swiss, with dovetailed joints.

The Oppenheimer cabin in the Pecos wilderness. Photo credit: Ed Reid

General Groves, for his part, was very strict and efficient as the military boss of Los Alamos. He had ideas on how to make things go faster. Not all of them worked out, but one that did was his decision to hire a workforce to take care of the general maintenance of the secret city. This would free the scientists from such responsibilities. Lacking this pressure, Groves thought the scientists would work day and night—and they did.

In 26 months, starting from scratch, these scientists and engineers developed and detonated two devices that changed the world. Only recently, with the effort to develop Covid vaccines, has a similar technical success been achieved in even less time. Arguably the threats to the world population from Nazi domination and an uncontrolled pandemic are comparable.

Chapter 3
Plutonium

Plutonium is the element that changed our lives. We had never heard the word for it was only first synthetically produced in December 1940 in Berkeley CA. Now, looking back, we realize that the force that had caught our family, moved us, and landed us in Los Alamos was plutonium, a heavy element that might be used to make another kind of atomic bomb. In 1939 scientists knew about refining uranium 235 to make a bomb. But then they realized that another element below uranium on the periodic table called plutonium, could be made to fission. Thus it might be possible to make two types of atomic bombs, one using uranium, the other, plutonium. That turned out to be easier said than done.

Plutonium, generated in nuclear reactors, can be made more efficiently than the refined uranium 235 being made at Oak Ridge. However, plutonium is a much more difficult bomb material to explode than uranium 235. One was hard to make (U235), the other was hard to detonate, (Pu).

That was a serious problem: how to make the plutonium explode. In 1942, scientists had only tiny amounts of plutonium with which to experiment. So Groves built a huge factory, Hanford, near Richland in Washington State, for making plutonium. They thought it would work pretty much like uranium. However, when they got significant quantities from Hanford, they learned to their dismay that plutonium did not behave like uranium. The "gun" mechanism intended to be used to detonate uranium wouldn't work. The uranium bomb was designed to be exploded by shooting one subcritical mass down a naval gun barrel into another subcritical mass at the end of the barrel quickly enough to produce what is known as a critical mass. But this would not work with the plutonium from the reactors at Hanford. This was because plutonium is much more radioactive than uranium. It would not be possible to shoot one subcritical mass into another subcritical mass quickly enough to assemble a critical mass. Only a small reaction would take place as the bomb would blow itself apart before the two subcritical parts were joined in the gun. The bomb would fissile. They had enough plutonium to create a critical mass but didn't know how to make it explode. They could not detonate it.

This was a low point in the project. After many discussions, they decided they had to design a new kind of detonator. And they needed a special team to do that. After only a short time at Oak Ridge, Daddy was interviewed and recruited by then Navy Commander Norris Bradbury (who much later became my father-in-law when I married his son John). Daddy was dispatched to Los Alamos, New Mexico to work on the problem.

The race to figure out how to detonate plutonium was on. And that was what Daddy and the other men in his group were there to do.

Norris Bradbury was looking for men who knew something about explosives, so I don't know why he picked Daddy. He was far from an expert in explosives. I suppose he was picked because he was smart. When he arrived at

Los Alamos, the laboratory was reorganizing and concentrating on figuring out how to detonate plutonium.

In early 1945 Daddy had a short interview with Oppenheimer who drew two concentric circles on his blackboard. He explained that the outer circle was high explosive (HE) material, the inner circle was plutonium. Oppie, as he was commonly known, said that the task was to explode the HE so as to compress the plutonium core to such an extent that it would become "critical" and explode. Daddy told Oppenheimer that he didn't know how to do this. "Neither do I," Oppenheimer told him. "You figure it out." That was the end of the interview and the beginning of the development of what became known as the high explosive lens.

Chapter 4
Los Alamos
The Secret City
Dorothy McKibbin

(See Appendix 7 for an article written by Dorothy McKibben about her job at Santa Fe.)

Almost immediately after Oppenheimer arrived in Santa Fe in the spring of 1943 as the new director of the Manhattan Project, he hired Dorothy McKibbin, a 42-year-old widow who knew almost everybody and everything in Santa Fe. Introduced to Oppenheimer in the lobby of La Fonda Hotel in Santa Fe, Dorothy was the perfect choice to help run the project.

McKibben ran her office from 109 East Palace (PO Box 1663), Santa Fe, New Mexico. She sent scientists, like Daddy with wives and tearful children up the rough and dusty road to Los Alamos.

Later Dottie said: "I thought to be associated with Oppenheimer would be simply great! I never met a person with a magnetism that hit you so fast and so completely as his did. I didn't know what he did. I thought maybe if he were digging trenches to put in a new road, I would love to do that, or if he were soliciting ads for a magazine or something, I would love to do that. I just wanted to be allied and have something to do with a person of such vitality and radiant force."

By early 1944 McKibbin found herself responsible for fixing everything - people, broken hearts, and lost pets or luggage. Everybody who was assigned to Los Alamos first reported to her tiny office in an old adobe building at the back of a small patio, just off the Santa Fe Plaza.

Frances Schulkin, a WAC assigned to the Manhattan Project, reported that this is what Dorothy was instructed to tell all new arrivals:

> This is a secret project. You cannot write or talk to outsiders about where you are stationed or what you do. You say you're with the engineers in Santa Fe. Period! Your mail will be censored, incoming and outgoing, so you better be careful about what you write. You will have your picture taken and get a badge. Because of security restrictions, civilians here cannot open checking accounts locally. Your paycheck will be sent to your home bank. There is a check-cashing service. If you go on a business trip there is a revolving fund of $100,000 to be used for travel accounting. Most people never get to Santa Fe because of security restrictions. You can't just pick up and go whenever you feel like it.

Later, as the project grew, this was added: "For security reasons the place of birth for all babies is P.O. Box 1663, Santa Fe, New Mexico." Eighty babies were born at Los Alamos in the first year.

Dorothy McKibbin, Robert Oppenheimer, and Victor Weisskopf at Oppenheimer's Bathtub Row house. Source: Courtesy of Los Alamos National Labs (LANL).

Los Alamos was never very militaristic and almost immediately generated domestic crisis after crisis. McKibbin was always cheery and resourceful, brushing away military procedures and dispatching people on to Los Alamos with badges (you had to have a badge, which showed you had a security clearance, to get through the Military Police who guarded the front gate to the Secret City). Her instructions were simple: "Please sit down, the MPs will pick you up right here, or you can drive, but the road is pretty bad." The road was so bad that one wife, after her first harrowing climb up to the top of the mesa, declared that she would just stay up there until the war was over.

That road wound through the Indian reservations of Tesuque and San Ildefonso, over the Rio Grande and then climbed up two very steep hills cut into the volcanic cliffs of the Jemez Mountains. It was not paved, often developed deep potholes, and was always dusty. It was marked by empty beer cans and no signs. Dorothy sent everyone off with simple directions like: "You can't miss it."

Many years later I lived with Dorothy for a few months and heard some of her stories. At one point, she told me, the security people at Los Alamos got worried that one of the project scientists might have had too much to drink at the bar in Santa Fe's best hotel, La Fonda. They held a meeting to decide if the bartender should be given authority to arrest or somehow silence the man to prevent him from spilling any secrets. Dorothy listened for a moment and said: "You are in a hotel. Just take that man upstairs and check him into one of your nice rooms, and then you take his pants off. He won't be back."

Los Alamos had been chosen because of its remote, beautiful location and because Oppenheimer loved it. He knew it was the perfect place for the campus of the small, secret laboratory he was going to direct. In the fall of 1942, the government purchased an elite school for boys, The Los Alamos Ranch School on the Pajarito Plateau in the Jamez Mountains. The site had spectacular views and a few log buildings that Oppenheimer thought would be adequate for their needs. Oppie, naively at first, thought that they could get by with maybe two outside phone lines and one for internal calls, and just six scientists. He greatly underestimated the task. Ultimately there were so many PhDs that General Groves made a rule that nobody was to

17

be called "doctor" because that could make the spies suspicious. Only medical doctors could be addressed as "doctor."

In 1943, when the Oppenheimers moved to Los Alamos with their young son, Peter, they moved into a house on what was called "Bathtub Row" because it was the only housing at Los Alamos that had bathtubs. These were log houses, not cabins, which had been built for the headmasters of the Ranch School while the boys lived outside on screened-in porches. Bathtub Row had real houses with yards, apricot and apple trees, lilacs, grass, and perhaps most importantly, bathtubs.

As soon as the first scientists arrived, the housing crisis began. Some of the luckiest senior scientists were assigned houses on Bathtub Row. But immediately it was clear that there were not enough houses for the scientists, let alone the support staff and everybody else who was arriving at Los Alamos.

Happy family in a Sundt apartment. The little boy is my friend Mike Haley. Photos such as these were an attempt to make life at Los Alamos look normal.

Everybody else lived in dorms or in the Sundt apartments that had so-called Black Beauty stoves which became famous because they did not work easily or very well or sometimes at all. Apartment heating was either off or on and never the right temperature. The Sundt apartments, with the infamous black cook stoves, were the first of a parade of every kind of prefabricated housing that sprawled over the mesa. The new houses were named after the contractors who built them—McKee, Denver Steel, Morgan, Quonset—and there were also all sorts of trailers. Every new house in Los Alamos was prefabricated, hauled up the hill in parts and quickly assembled, and although they varied somewhat in style, everyone had only a cramped metal shower stall. These showers were very unpopular. When we finally got a house in Los Alamos, I was terrified of the shower, and had nightmares about it.

But by the time we arrived, the housing crisis had gotten worse. There was no place for us to live.

Chapter 5
Living in a Tent

Our parents were educated, upper-middle-class Kentucky southerners on both sides. Both came from big families. Mother was a chemist and Daddy was a chemical engineer. Mother taught school until she and Daddy married. Before we moved to New Mexico, we lived in Louisville, where, I am sure, my parents thought they would remain for the rest of their lives. When Mother told our ancient Great Aunts, Aunt Pealie and Aunt Bertie, that we were moving to New Mexico, they were horrified, sure that Indians would kill us. It was the first mention of Indians I had ever heard, and I wanted to know more about them. Such information was never going to come from Aunt Pealie and Aunt Bertie, whose fixed opinions, based on attendance at "wild west" shows, were not to be disputed.

Mother was the oldest child of a family that had a small plantation, called the Meadows, outside of Louisville. After the Civil War, many of the former slaves came back to where they had lived before the war. They were no longer slaves but were welcomed back.

As a small child, the only war I ever heard anyone talk about was the Civil War, so I confused the Civil War with World War II. When Roosevelt died, someone phoned my grandmother, and I heard her say "Oh, dear. . . ." I then asked her if that meant the Yankees had won the war.

My favorite story was about when some Yankees came to my great-great-grandmother's kitchen and demanded that they be given breakfast. She took one look at the small group of bedraggled men and announced, "If there is a gentleman among you, I will speak to him." They all trooped out and returned with an officer, in dress uniform, sword at his side, clearly a gentleman and he asked very politely. So she served them breakfast. This is a telling story about how close the sides were to each other—having breakfast and then going on killing each other.

Daddy's family also had a plantation, called Bashford Manor, which was built after the Civil War on the proceeds of a patent medicine called Wilder's Worm Syrup. It was supposed to make workers work faster. Daddy said he thought it tasted so bad that people worked harder so they wouldn't have to take it. It was a secret formula.

We lived in a small house on Finley Avenue in Louisville. I had a room upstairs and Marshall had one downstairs. Life was pleasant. My ambition was to invent a new color. Daddy told me that there were more colors, like in rainbows, but that you couldn't see them. I didn't think that made sense, since what good is a color if you can't see it?

Mother, Marshall, and Ellen in Kentucky before going to New Mexico.

When Daddy got the call to serve in the military, like most Americans he responded without hesitation. I described earlier how his background and credentials led to his being assigned to officer training and ultimately Los Alamos. Families in this situation often faced the prospect of months and years of separation from their loved ones. But not at Los Alamos. As I've already mentioned, the Manhattan Project allowed men to have their families with them. Then Mother got a phone call from Betty Wilson, the wife of another Navy man, Bill Wilson, who was also headed to the unknown somewhere out west. So these two Navy families decided to drive together to this mysterious place. That included Mother, my little brother, Marshall, who was three years old, Betty Wilson and her kids, Billy and Sis, and a young man who knew how to change tires. Tires were fragile because the war effort had priority on rubber, and blowouts were frequent. All of us were packed into the Wilsons' Buick Roadmaster: three adults and four kids under six with gas rationing and an uncertain destination thrown into the mix. This was early spring of 1945.

I was sad because I had to leave my pet rabbit, Funny Bunny. I remember that trip because I sat behind the driver and at one point, because I was bored or wanted to experiment, I cranked the window up with my chin resting on it, until it got stuck. For some reason I couldn't crank the window down. My head was clamped between the window and the window frame, and I couldn't talk. I could squeak, but maybe all the kids in the backseat were also squeaking, so nobody noticed. Anyway, we rode along for miles and still nobody noticed I hadn't spoken for what seemed to me a long time. The worst was when we stopped and I didn't get out. I couldn't, and when they figured out what was wrong, they all laughed at me. Maybe I talked too much, because I was very interested in everything, and they had been happy for a reprieve. I still have a scar where the window caught my chin.

After three or more days driving, we finally arrived in Santa Fe at Dorothy McKibbin's office, which was heated—or not heated—by a small fireplace. There were a couch and desk, two telephones—one line had been borrowed from the Forest Service because phone lines were difficult to come by in those days—and there was a sort of patio in front with a big pile of suitcases and bags. Dorothy's office was right opposite the U.S. Post Office, where mail for Los Alamos had the P.O. Box number 1663. Then we were told the bad news. There was no place for us to live in Los Alamos. All the housing was already taken.

Someone suggested that we might find a motel in Albuquerque, 60 miles south of Santa Fe and a hundred miles south of Los Alamos. So we drove to Albuquerque and moved into the De Anza Motel. For a few weeks our fathers drove down every weekend. This took a lot of gas at a time when gas was rationed.

The motel had no place to cook and the only place for us kids to play was outside. It was dusty. I remember playing outside in dirt baked to a solid block by the sun, getting filthy, getting fussed at. Inside I don't think there was any air conditioning. I have no idea how Mother cooked anything.

Probably because Daddy and Bill Wilson were driving back and forth every weekend, they were always followed by another car, most likely the FBI that thought bomb scientists with permission to leave the top-secret Lab were possible spies. As soon as they exited the main gate of Los Alamos, where their passes were checked, the car with two men pulled in behind them and followed them all the way to the De Anza motel.

Eventually, frustrated and using precious gas, Daddy and Bill Wilson decided that we would just camp in nearby Frijoles Canyon in Bandelier National Monument. The park had been closed because there were very few tourists during the war and it was too close to the Lab, and to S-Site, where they worked. They had heard that there might be a few cabins available in Bandelier.

Our campsite in Frijoles Canyon. Mother and I are in front of the Wilder tent.
Photo credit: Kay Wilson Martin

In 1944 Dorothy McKibbin had convinced Evelyn Frey, who ran a little tourist lodge in the park, which included Frijoles Canyon, to let some of the rapidly expanding population of Los Alamos live in a few of the small guesthouses that had been constructed by the Works Progress Administration (WPA) during the Depression. But when we got there, we learned these guesthouses had been ordered closed by the authorities at Los Alamos perhaps due to security and safety concerns because they were too close to S-Site.

However, Bandelier also had a nice campground that had also been constructed by the WPA. It was in deep, verdant Frijoles Canyon. There were tall trees over-hanging the little creek, picnic tables, and water for campers. It was cool and deserted. After three weeks in a tiny hot motel in Albuquerque, my parents and the Wilsons decided that we would just camp—without permission from Los Alamos security.

I thought it was idyllic. The little stream was full of fish. We were close to prehistoric cliff dwellings cut into the soft volcanic tuff from the Valle Grande Caldera, an extinct volcano that exploded about 1.2 million years ago. We lived in a big white tent in the bottom of the canyon. This was close to where Daddy worked at S-Site, named for a sawmill that had been there. This was very convenient for him since S-Site was where Daddy's team was testing the conventional explosives that they hoped would work to detonate the implosion bomb. It was separated from the town because of the work with high explosives. We got very used to the regular explosions.

It was May and the nights were chilly. We needed kapok sleeping bags. Inside the tent we had a tarp on the floor and slept on cots. Mother, who had a cook when she lived in Louisville, made every meal on a camp stove or over the open campfire. Somehow, she was able to iron Daddy's kaki Navy uniforms with an iron that was heated either on the camp stove or over the fire without grinding ashes into the uniform.

I thought it was fun. We had free run of the canyon. We were the only kids there. We played in the stream. It's a wonder that none of us were ever hurt—except for me when my thumb was smashed.

Sometimes as kids we would wander over to the Indian ruins that had been abandoned about 1550 AD. Among the artifacts we explored were kivas. A kiva is a round, steeply walled hole in the ground, perhaps twenty-five feet in diameter and four-to-five feet deep. This was a prehistoric Indian religious center used by Puebloans for rites and political meetings, often connected to the Kachina belief system. In modern Hopi and Pueblo contexts, kiva means a large, circular, underground room used for spiritual ceremonies.

When the indigenous people lived in the canyon kivas had a roof, but they all had collapsed long ago. Once, like a big sister, I pushed Marshall into one of the kivas. It was not very deep, and Marshall sat in the sand at the bottom and cried. He later said he thought that he might have to stay in that kiva forever since I evidently was not likely to help him out or tell anyone where he was. This was an accurate assessment of the situation. I had walked back to camp by myself, where Mother asked, "Where is Marshall?" At first I said I didn't know, but that didn't work, so I said he fell into the kiva. That did not help my story. Pushing him into the kiva had seemed like a good idea at the time. Marshall was rescued, unhurt but unhappy.

Top: The kiva that I pushed Marshall into, which did not have a roof. Bottom: A restored kiva in the Ceremonial cave. Source: Bandelier web site.

It was quite a life. We had a log picnic table in our campsite along with the tent and the run of the canyon. We had two cars, the Wilsons' and ours. The men took one car to work, but gas rationing kept us in the canyon. As Mother said, it was wartime and we all wanted to do everything we could to help with the effort.

Our sleeping bags were arranged on cots around the inside of the tent. Skunks prowled outside at night, looking for ways to get under the sides of the tent. One night a skunk actually got into the tent and wandered right under my cot. Daddy hissed at us to be very quiet, and we were, while the skunk rummaged around and finally left. After that Daddy skunk-proofed the tent with logs tucked under the edges of the canvas sides.

Down the road from our campsite there was a "comfort station" with big showers, restrooms, and daddy longlegs spiders all over the place. I thought it was creepy and dangerous. I didn't want to take a shower. I wanted to wash in the creek but was told that would be bad for the fish. I liked the fish, so I thought I would just go without washing. We shared the park with three rangers and a local shepherd who lived in another tent downstream from us. It was pretty much us and the local wildlife. Speaking of skunks, one night two of them got into the shepherd's tent and had a fight. We walked past his place the next day. Whew. We learned to be very careful about skunks.

Besides skunks there were squirrels which ran down the trees and stole our bread and anything else they could carry. There wasn't much we could do about the squirrels. They scampered around and picked up anything left on the picnic tables. I spent a lot of time up a tree I shared with a squirrel, which chattered and fussed at me, but I thought it was my tree, too. I spent pretty much the entire summer sitting in a tree with a squirrel that did not want to share his tree.

In my favorite tree. I think I am dressed like Tarzan.

When it rained, the tent floor filled with water, and sometimes Mrs. Frey, the owner of the tourist lodge, took us into her house. She had a small cottage where she kept the room that had belonged to her son who had been killed in the war. It was just as he left it. We couldn't go into that room. She was very nice, and when we got a house at Los Alamos she gave me a rosebush called the Seven Sisters which I kept for many years. When we stayed with her, we could sit out of the rain in a dry place and she and Mother talked and had tea.

We shopped in the not very nearby town of Española where there were two general stores, Peoples and Bond-Willards. One clerk spoke English. Not many people in Española spoke English. Rather, they spoke Spanish or Tewa, the language of the Indians from Santa Clara Pueblo. Once in the Wilsons' car we had a small accident and then *nobody* spoke English, even if they could, except a guy at Hunter Motors who came over to make sure there was no damage. There wasn't. Betty Wilson had run into a truck in the middle of a big open area. Neither vehicle was going very fast, and no one was hurt.

Everything was supposed to be very secret at Los Alamos, but while we were living in the tent Daddy told me they were making a new weapon, something that had never been invented before. He said it was going to be a bomb. I was concerned because I knew bombs had already been invented. I thought he might get in trouble if he didn't make something better than a bomb. Maybe I could help my father's effort by inventing something really new.

So I spent a lot of time at camp trying to get a lizard to walk through the campfire. I thought it would turn into some sort of huge dragon, a sort of proto-Godzilla. I don't know where I got this idea. I spent a lot of my time at camp coaching lizards into the fire with small sticks. For weeks I worked hard on this lizard-herding project that I thought would be more effective than a bomb. Finally, one day, using twigs, I managed to herd a lizard into the ashes of the fireplace. I had done it and I was terrified.

31

I knew that if my plan really worked, the dragon I created would eat my family. Like so many who make weapons, I realized that I didn't know how to control my creation. I raced down to the park headquarters and begged the park ranger to run back to our campsite with me and kill the huge dragon that I knew was going to emerge from the ashes. The ranger followed me, but he would not run. I was so frantic that I ran ahead, only to find everyone was just fine and there was no lizard of any size. I was very much relieved.

This put a damper on my career as a weapons developer.

The same ranger later told me not to go up a path that led to a large ceremonial cave upstream from our camp. Naturally the next day I set off up the path. I had never been very far from our camp before and didn't know where the trail went. But I wasn't supposed to go there, so clearly it must be an interesting destination. Marching along, I looked up and saw a big mountain lion looking down at me. She was on top of a big rock, just about four feet above my head. A big old mountain lion. Maybe she could no longer hunt very well; a small girl might be delicious.

The lion and I looked at each other and I decided I should slowly walk on. Somehow, I knew I should not run, and I walked slowly past the lion. However, once past her and around a bend in the trail, I didn't know how to get back to our campsite unless I walked back past the lion again, which I really didn't want to do. But how else could I get back to camp?

I turned around and walked very slowly past the lion again. She turned her head to look at me, but she didn't move. I walked very slowly until I was well past her, and then I ran as fast as I could. I got back to the park headquarters and found the ranger. Breathlessly I told him there was a mountain lion on that path. He said, "Well, that's why I told you not to go up there." But, I pointed out, you didn't tell me *why* I shouldn't go.

One afternoon, probably a Sunday, because Daddy was there (the scientists and engineers developing the bomb worked six days a week), we were playing in the creek in Frijoles. Marshall and I usually just waded in and tried to catch the fish where they were hiding under the banks, but that day we were both throwing rocks at the fish. The fish were safe; we were not very good at aiming the rocks. Marshall threw a big rock that hit my left thumb and squashed it. He said he didn't do it on purpose; I am not too sure.

It was smashed. It bled, it hurt, and it looked awful. I cried. Daddy decided to take me up to Los Alamos to the hospital to have them look at it. We drove up to the back gate which was near S-Site. He went through that gate every day, but not this day. The guard, who was probably about eighteen years old, would not let me in because I didn't have a pass. You had to have a pass. He had orders.

Daddy had a pass but that would not get *me* in. The guard said no, I could not go to the hospital without a pass. But he gave me some candy. It was mint, not a kind I liked, but I ate some because I could see he was sorry for me, and I didn't want to hurt his feelings. He was a nice guy, but he had orders.

I don't think I had ever seen my father so angry before. After some minutes, Daddy persuaded the guard that even though I did not have a security clearance and a pass, he could let me in and take me to the hospital. I asked Daddy why they wouldn't let me in. "Because we are doing something really secret." I thought it probably was something better than a bomb. Something *really* interesting.

Back Gate. Photo credit to Getty Images

I decided I would get even with them for not letting me in. I would figure out the secret and then tell everybody. I didn't think that a bomb could be the secret since Daddy had already told me about that, and bombs had already been invented.

We drove to the Los Alamos hospital, and they bandaged my thumb. While we were there, I looked all around to see what the secret could be. It all looked pretty boring except for some ducks on a pond behind a fence. I thought that must be it, the secret: There were eleven ducks. I could count that high. And they were behind a tall fence. I knew that everything behind the fence was top secret which proved to me that the ducks were important.

I didn't see anything else that looked very interesting. All the buildings were dark green boxes with fences all around. It didn't look like anything that might be a very good secret except for the ducks in a pond behind a fence. I resolved to tell, as soon as I could. Eleven ducks. Kept behind a fence. What fun is a secret if you can't tell anybody? But I didn't know who to tell.

My thumb healed, though today is still smaller than my other one. We went on picking fish out of the stream. Daddy taped sandpaper to our fingers so we could hold onto the fish. It just didn't make sense to use a pole if you could just pick them up.

All of this was going on in the foreground for me, but for Daddy it was probably a big distraction. His main focus had to be on his work at S-Site developing a way to detonate the plutonium bomb.

Chapter 6
Daddy and the Detonator

"If you see me running, just try to keep up."
—Safety procedures at S-Site

By Mid-July of 1945 the United States had built two bombs: one using uranium 235 and the other using plutonium. The plutonium bomb, nicknamed Fat Man, had a spherical shell with two polar caps and five equatorial zone sheets surrounded by another shell. All the electrical detonating and fusing equipment to initiate the implosion was mounted in the space between the bomb sphere and the outer shell. Norris Bradbury was in charge of research. Kenneth Bainbridge oversaw development engineering and testing for implosion. George Kistiakowsky was responsible for casting the explosive charges.

S-Site, where Daddy was assigned and where the explosives work was done, consumed over 50,000 pounds of explosives in one month.

"Our responsibility," Daddy wrote, "was to develop and manufacture the high explosive system for the implosion bomb. Nobody had ever done anything like this before."*

The site was and still is remote from the Los Alamos town site. They knew detonating lots of high explosives would be dangerous work. Finally by testing different explosive materials and shapes, they figured out how to successfully fabricate the high explosive (HE) lens that would compress and detonate the plutonium. Their work paid off when the world's first atomic bomb was tested on

July 16,1945 at the Trinity site about 200 miles south of Los Alamos.

S-Site was so secret that a book written and published in 1945, *Atomic Energy for Military Purposes* by Henry DeWolf Smyth, recounted in great detail how the bombs were developed by the Manhattan Project – but scarcely mentioned S-Site. In my father's copy of this book, which Marshall got when Daddy died in 1997, Daddy made a note on page 222, which is shown below. It contains the book's single mention of the work done at S-Site, despite its importance and the book's level of detail. The note in the margin of the page is in Daddy's handwriting. The note says, "This covers my work."

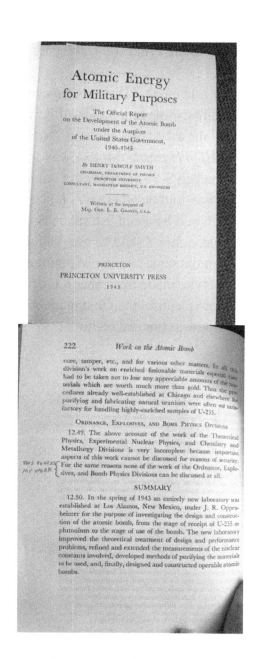

Title page and page 222 of Daddy's copy of *Atomic Energy for Military Purposes*,

38

Henry DeWolf Smyth, Princeton University Press, 1945.

Later Mother told me that Daddy's paycheck always had an "H" on it. She thought it indicated *health insurance.* Many years later she asked him about it. "No," he told her. "That indicated *High Hazard.*" Mother was shocked.

Daddy also had an S-Site story about requesting some copper wire. He was told that there was no copper available. He then said he could use silver. Sorry, there was no silver available, either. Could he use platinum? Yes, he said, and was sent the same amount of platinum. The irony of wartime—that wire made from one of the rarest elements was more plentiful than that made from a common element—was not lost on him.

The Navy explosive engineering team. Back of the jeep left to right: Wm. A. Wilson, Muncy, Sullivan, John H. Russell. Front row: Brenan, Edward Wilder, Gordon C. Chappell.

Not present: Norm Gilbert. The sign is a joke, since the work at S-Site was very secret, although it is hard to keep explosions secret.

Drawing by John Hull. They are assembling the high explosive lens sections. The caption reads: Ed Wilder and Bill Wilson assemble the Gadget at V-site for the Trinity Test, July 1945

Edward Wilder on Fat Man.
This highly classified unauthorized photograph was
declassified and given to Daddy upon his retirement from
the Lab in 1970. If you look closely at the writing above
Bugs Bunny, it says "HIGH EXPLOSIVES
DANGEROUS." We don't know how this photograph was
taken but it was likely with a professional camera. This and
the picture of the engineers in the jeep show that the young
men doing this dangerous and very important work had a
well-developed sense of humor.

When the scientists at Los Alamos planned to move the
precious plutonium bomb core to Trinity Site for the big
test, they wanted to do it under cover of darkness to avoid
attention. When they notified Santa Fe Police that a small

important convoy was scheduled to drive through town about midnight, the police said no. Absolutely not, too dangerous. That was when most drunk drivers decided to drive home, making it the worst time possible. But all arrangements and schedules had been made, so the police decided, in the interest of safety, to provide an escort. They surrounded the super secret convoy with police cars, sirens screaming, lights flashing and horns blaring to escort them to the outskirts of Santa Fe. There the original plan went back into effect and they arrived at Trinity without incident.

(Top) At the Trinity site, Herb Leir carrying the magnesium case containing the plutonium core. (Bottom) Closeup of the case. Note the round thermometer on the top and the rubber bumpers on the side and bottom. Source: Los Alamos National Laboratory

Appendix 3 includes the details of the delivery of the bomb components to the remote Pacific Island of Tinian.

In early August 1945 Daddy came home and told us to get in the car so we could listen to the radio. We were going to hear something very important. Our only radio was in the car, so we climbed in. I sat on the floor by my mother's feet. I did not want to miss this important thing. We listened to the limited-power Los Alamos radio station, KRS. They broadcast an early "wire" recording from the cockpit of the Enola Gay, the B-29 bomber that had dropped the first atomic bomb.

What we heard was the roar of the engines, then the countdown: "10, 9, 8, 7, 6, 5, 4, 3, 2, 1, bombs away," and then the clatter of metal when the shock wave hit the plane, and then a boom, the sound of the explosion. I believe that this wire recording has been lost.

I was really impressed. That man could count backwards! I had never thought of such a thing. I still remember that seemed to me a much bigger deal, since explosions were pretty commonplace. It wouldn't be until much later that I even began to understand the significance of that day.

Notes for further reading

*This quotation is from "Description of the work done at S-Site" by Edward Wilder, which was written after much of the work done during World War II at Los Alamos was partially declassified. It was published as an appendix in *Manhattan District History: Nonscientific Aspects of Los*

Alamos Project Y, 1942 through 1946. Edited by Kasha V. Thayer. Published by the Los Alamos Historical Society, Los Alamos, New Mexico. The article appears in the present volume as Appendix 1.

Also included in this volume, as Appendix 2, is: George B. Kistiakowsky, "Trinity—A Reminiscence," originally published in *The Bulletin of the Atomic Scientists*, volume 36, issue 6, 1980.

Appendix 3 is an article about dropping Fat Man on Nagasaki. This was written by Ellen Bradbury-Reid and Paula Schreiber Dransfield. Paula was the daughter of Raemer Schrieber, one of the main PhD scientists responsible for much of the bomb development work at Los Alamos. Schreiber kept a diary, which Paula and I used as reference for this article.

Appendix 4 is a short article by Richard Rhodes about the debate surrounding the dropping of the bombs on Japan, and Oppenheimer's prediction concerning the long term effects on future wars of doing so.

Here is a link to an excellent in-depth piece on the efforts and effects of the development of the bomb.
https://youtu.be/1y1jGZnzB7U

Chapter 7
Life in Los Alamos

By the end of World War II housing in Los Alamos became available as many scientists returned to their previous positions in academia or industry. My parents liked New Mexico and Los Alamos, so we stayed. We were assigned a McKee house. This was a prefabricated box house with a white picket fence around a small empty yard—an illusion of some other place. And the shower—I hated the shower, which was cramped and made of a dark tin-like metal. And it smelled funny, wet, and funky.

The housing area was adjacent to the Technical Area which was in the center of town and included the pond. A fence separated the Technical Area from town, and the entire town was also surrounded by a larger security fence. So there were two fences and you had to show a pass to get in or out of the big fence with barbed wire on top, which encircled everything. The town area itself was small, and you could walk everywhere.

McKee House. Source: The Manhattan District History, Nonscientific Aspects of Los Alamos Project Y. 1942 through 1946. Written by Edith C. Truslow and edited by Kasa V. Thayer. Available from National Technical Information Service 5285 Port Royal Road, Springfield, Virginia 22151 Issued March 1973.

The Jemez mountains behind Los Alamos and the nearby Sangre de Cristo Mountain range were great for climbing and skiing. George Kistiakowsky, the great Ukrainian explosives expert and Daddy's boss, blew up enough trees to clear a ski run near S-Site. (Blowing them up was easier and more fun than cutting them down.) A pond located at the bottom of a nearby steep canyon was used as a skating rink in winters which were, and are still cold. As children, Marshall and I spent many hours after school ice skating there and many hours after that trying to warm up our feet.

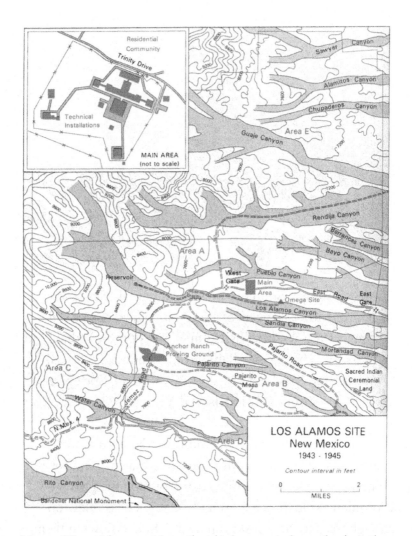

Map of Los Alamos. Note that it does not show the location of S-Site.

These super-stressed and very busy people also produced theatricals. I think the arrival of the British physicists helped raise the thespian standards. Skits and even Gilbert and Sullivan operettas were eventually produced. For years I thought the famous physicist British James Tuck, who had a good singing voice, was either the Captain of the Pinafore or the Pirate King. Even Oppie appeared as a corpse in *Arsenic and Old Lace*.

For years after the end of the Manhattan Project there was a New Year's Eve event called the Newcomers Party. To be invited you had to have come to Los Alamos before the end of the war. It usually had a skit that related to some part of the Lab, often a stepladder with a bucket that they could not knock off that represented a Tower Test, like Trinity, but one that didn't work.

In the loose communal atmosphere Oppenheimer developed, meals were often served at the Fuller Lodge where social as well as professional meetings took place. This wonderful old building was designed by Santa Fe architect John Gaw Meem with vertical logs, a big center room and a balcony with surrounding rooms. This building was and still is the center of Los Alamos life.

Fuller Lodge. Source: *The Manhattan District History, Nonscientific Aspects of Los Alamos Project Y. 1942 through 1946.* Written by Edith C. Truslow and edited by Kasa V. Thayer. Available from National Technical Information Service 5285 Port Royal Road, Springfield, Virginia 22151 Issued March 1973.

Françoise Ulam, the wife of Stan Ulam, the co-inventor of the hydrogen bomb, thought the atmosphere was like a summer camp. She, being French and fashion-conscious, noted that people wore plaid shirts. People were indeed casually dressed given that the place was always dusty. And besides, there was no place to go that called for fancier dress. Oppie wore blue work shirts and cowboy boots. Most people wore jeans. Eleanor Jette remembered: "Daytimes, men and women alike went about in bright gingham shirts with slacks or blue jeans." (From *Inside Box 1663*. Published by the Los Alamos Historical Society 1977.) Square dancing was popular in the evenings. For parties, though, the style was more formal. The men dressed in business suits and women took out their hoarded pre-war nylons and best navy-blue dresses. Black ties and evening gowns dominated the big parties.

As kids we thought that the Indian women who were picked up every morning in trucks with little houses built over the truck beds were lucky. We wanted to ride in one of those neat little houses. These maids, from San Ildefonso and Santa Clara pueblos were mostly not familiar with washing machines, vacuum cleaners or other "labor saving." devices. So they would not use some but were fascinated by, say, the washing machine with a little glass window on its door. The women were kind and invited us to visit on their feast days when they would dance and feed everyone. They made little clay bears and turtles for us to play with. And to the dismay of many scientists wives, the maids had minds of their own. When they were assigned to a house where they didn't like the people, they often went over to the houses where they did like the people. Since there were no telephones, if your maid did not show up, you had to go from house to house looking for her.

The accounts of the very early days of living at Los Alamos, mostly by women, are filled with dry stiff upper lip sort of humor. The excitement of meeting Nobel prize winners and having maids and finding that whiskey was nearly impossible to find wore thin. Our parents learned to square dance. We went to Fiesta in Santa Fe to watch the burning of Zozobra, a 40-foot puppet that was burned every September to get rid of the evils and gloom of the past year. This was all very exciting; fireworks, groans, a fire dancer. It was also very scary since in those days spectators' cars were allowed to park almost right under

50

Zozobra's robe. He had a finger that pointed right at you. He had loud groans. Marshall tried to hide on the car's floor under the back seat.

Zozobra, also known as Old Man Gloom. Picture from Santa Fe web site.

Later we noticed there were some peculiar aspects to Los Alamos parties. Claire Ulam, Françoise and Stan's daughter, told an interviewer once that as a child she thought what happened at parties was that the men all went to a corner and talked. Parties were just another opportunity to hash out the most recent problem. At the Bradbury's house, the men always went down to the barbeque to talk. That was normal. Well, not really, but that was the way parties at Los Alamos worked. Was it because they didn't want to be overheard? Or maybe they thought the houses were bugged? The FBI bugged Oppenheimer's house in San Francisco. But the FBI were not allowed into Los Alamos. Anyway, it was the way parties went.

The Army ran the town, but the community was vocal and not at all used to the military's idea of organization. The Army, or maybe it was General Groves specifically, decided that apartments were to be assigned according to the number of children in the family. Generally, the maintenance people had more kids than the physicist families which resulted in some surprising democracy. Maintenance men lived above famous physicists. Never the less, they all seemed to get along.

There was a common effort to help newcomers with the various problems caused by living in a place that did not exist to the outside world. No relatives could visit, letters were censored and there were no telephones, but you could have pets. Or maybe they had just not gotten around to forbidding them. One of our neighbors had a horse, dogs, and I think a goat. I was impressed. I just asked for a kitten but was told no.

Children living at Los Alamos were required to get a pass and a security clearance at age six. General Groves must have decided that six year olds could probably read and talk, and so might be a security risk—which was exactly what I wanted to be as I pursued my spying career.` At the same time, however, I needed that security clearance because I wanted to go on living with my parents. I knew that you couldn't live in Los Alamos without a pass. I wasn't sure where spies lived, but probably not with their parents.

Getting a pass to go into Los Alamos was a very big deal. You went to the badge office where they took your picture, fingerprints, and gave you a number. Mine was Z14020. All kids wanted to have a pass. The counter in the office was too high for us six-year-olds, so my mother had to hold me up so they could take a fingerprint. My finger came back black from the ink. It was exciting. I was thrilled.

This is a replacement pass given when I got older. My original pass from when I was six years old was kept by the badge office when I got the new one.

Mother's pass.

When Los Alamos was opened for anyone to enter, the security forces did not bother to collect residents' passes.

***

As the town of Los Alamos developed into a real community, with permanent housing, schools and shopping areas, it became apparent to the Government that there was no need to keep the town in a secure environment. The important security fences already surrounded the technical areas which were increasingly separated from the town. On February 18, 1957 the gates guarding the town came down.

The opening up of Los Alamos was noted in several of the area's newspapers. The Albuquerque Journal May 6, 1957, edition had the headline "Los Alamos Notes Little Effect from opening its Gates". Los Alamos residents were shocked in February 1957 to learn that in less than one week, the gates that guarded the town since its inception would come down. The town had been a top-secret city during World War II and a "gated" community since, and most residents were used to keeping their doors unlocked and their bicycles left out and about.

Prior to the opening of the gates visitors to Los Alamos had to obtain a pass at least 24 hours in advance of their arrival. They had to be visiting someone specific – no tourists or casual visitors were allowed. Out-of-town high school sports teams were required to have a pass for everyone on the bus.

"Los Alamos Throws Gate Wide Open", a Santa Fe New Mexican headline declared. The article went on to explain only three residents had contacted the Atomic Energy Commission about the decision, two in favor and one against.

There was still one big problem, though. An article in Newsweek magazine on March 4, 1957, lamented: "But the people of Los Alamos, as they looked around at their snug houses of pink, blue, green and white, weren't so sure they would like being more normal. Until now, they had not had to worry about burglars, hawkers, tourists, or even unexpected visits from in-laws.

Chapter 8
My Career as a Spy

After we moved from our tent at Bandelier to a house in
Los Alamos, I mourned the loss of trees. So I would walk
down Bathtub Row, where there were trees and grass to
escape the dust and mud. I remember that even bindweed,
a horrible pest, was precious because it was green, and had
little white flowers. I would kneel over a plant and cup my
hands around it, pretending there were more green things.
But there weren't. Bandelier was green, Kentucky had been
green, but Los Alamos was raw and except for Bathtub
Row, nothing was green.

Marshall, Daddy, Ellen with McKee house in background

Our little house was an improvement over the tent but not as much fun. I am sure that Mother was delighted. It had a bathroom, a kitchen, three tiny bedrooms, and from my point of view one very important career advantage. It was right next to the high wire fence that surrounded the Los Alamos Technical Area and I had not yet completed my career in espionage. I had not told my secret. I devoted much of my time to sitting next to that fence, waiting for someone who would like to know my secret: eleven ducks. But no one came by to ask me about the secret. It was disappointing, but I was not deterred. The MPs patrolling the fence would drive by in their jeeps and ask me what I was doing or if I was lost. But no, I was not lost, and I certainly could not tell them what I was doing. I was a spy.

Finally, I got really tired of sitting on the ground next to the fence every day and decided to do something about it. I was not going to go on waiting for someone to ask me about the secret. I got my little brother, Marshall, and pushed him into a culvert that went under the fence. I was already too big to crawl through but I thought he could escape because he was smaller than me.

My plan was that he could find someone, (I wasn't sure whom), I could tell my secret to, and then I could conclude my spying career and get a pass and continue to live with my family. But Marshall got his knees and elbows doubled up underneath him and was stuck inside the culvert. Of course, my plan had not allowed for the fact that he was only three and had not volunteered for this job. He started to cry. That is what three-year-old kids do when big sisters abuse them. He was really loud. And he was really stuck. He could not back out of the pipe. I tried but I couldn't pull him out of the culvert. I knew my plan was not going very well.

Then some of the MPs who patrolled the fence came by in a jeep and asked me what I was doing. I said nothing, but I knew this was getting worse, not working out at all. Then Mother came to see what was going on. Marshall was crying so loud she could probably hear him from the house. Finally, Daddy, who must have been summoned by the MPs, came to look at the situation.

I knew this was really going to be bad for me. I was sure Marshall would tell on me. Daddy grabbed Marshall by the legs and pulled him out of the pipe. He really cried a lot but luckily he was only upset and not really hurt. And luckily for me, he was so upset he didn't tell anyone how he got into the culvert, and no one thought to ask me. This had been a very narrow escape and I decided that espionage was just too dangerous for me.

And I got my pass, so I could keep on living with my family. The security of Los Alamos was intact (well, as we now know, it was not), no thanks to me.

Ellen age 8

***

As kids we listened to test explosions every day. They were
timed at 10, 12, and 3 o'clock so that everyone knew they
were not accidents. We liked big booms that produced a

puff of smoke and maybe rattled the windows. We were not afraid because they were regular, common, and meant recess, lunch, and time to go home. I guess we also had a school bell, but the explosions worked for us.

There was only one school in town, named Central School. We walked to it, came home for lunch and then walked back to school. Later I learned that Los Alamos paid their teachers more than any other teachers in New Mexico. They still do. It was important to have and keep good teachers because of the emphasis on education among the scientists. There were so many kids that we had two first grade teachers. Mine was Mrs. Tinsley. I just loved her, but I was so shy I would only whisper to her. I just didn't want to talk out loud. I don't think anybody paid any attention to me, which made me think I was invisible. I got over that somehow. I already knew how to read and was afraid that I might get into trouble if she found out. Maybe we were smart kids, but we also had good teachers and our parents all valued education.

By Christmas, with no special attention, almost everybody could read, and I stopped whispering. My third-grade class learned a Christmas carol that we sang to the tune of "Oh Tannenbaum": "Atomic Bomb, Atomic bomb . . . ." We all knew what that was.

I had a sort of boyfriend, Francis Dudley Williams III, who walked home with me. He once told my mother that he liked me, but I was not as interested in Zeus as he was. Mother thought this was funny. It might have been a stumbling block to our future together. Since we were both only six, though, I had some time to bone up on the Greek pantheon.

60

Maybe Los Alamos kids were a bit special because their parents certainly were.

Kids on army Jeep in the McKee area. I am the curly haired blond standing in the back. Photograph from the Los Alamos Historical Society.

My little sister, Carolyn, was born in June 1947. Her birth certificate is probably one of the first to actually say that the birth took place in a town called Los Alamos and not P.O. Box 1663, Sandoval County, New Mexico. General Groves was tearing his hair out at the number of babies born in P.O. Box 1663. He said that there were too many babies and kids. Groves ordered Oppenheimer to put a stop to it, but Oppie explained that was not his responsibility. At the time, Oppie's wife was pregnant with their second child.

There were no telephones and no cameras allowed inside the fence, so there are few photos from that time. The Army had confiscated all the cameras, most of which were Kodak Brownies, so after the war, when the cameras were returned, they just gave everybody a Brownie camera. Apparently, it was the only model available, so everybody had the same one.

At Los Alamos the military provided free medical care. The medical doctors were trained to treat soldiers wounded in battle, but were instead faced with a bunch of high-strung, healthy civilians with minor ailments, lots of older kids, like Marshall and me, and an incredible number of babies, already born or on the way. It cost a dollar to have a baby at Los Alamos, and almost everybody did. The first year, eighty babies were born in the hospital. My parents added to the number of babies by having Carolyn. I had not asked for a little sister; I still wanted a kitten.

Apparently, I asked for a kitten very persistently, so when my sister Carolyn was born, I got one. A kitten *and* a baby sister. I didn't know if she was a consolation prize—I had really just wanted a kitten, but it was okay to have a baby sister.

***

There was a nice stable at Los Alamos where the Army had kept their horses. Apparently the original plan was to import Kentucky thoroughbreds to patrol the fence. That did not work out because the temperamental horses were too delicate for the rough New Mexico terrain and were eventually shipped out. But the stables remained. This was nice, since the Oppenheimers both rode, and they had good horses. Martha Parson, Eleanor Jette and Kitty Oppenheimer sometimes took long distance afternoon rides into the mountains. Parsons husband, Deke was second-in-command at Los Alamos. He lived across the street from the Oppenheimers with his wife and daughter.

George Kistiakowsky bought a horse appropriately named Chaos from the Oppenheimers. Previously Oppie had a horse named Crisis. At first the stables were near the houses in town, but were eventually moved to what became the Western Area.

***

Because it was run by the military, Los Alamos had weekly parades. Early on, parades usually began with Timoshenko, a large Russian Wolfhound named for a famous Russian commander, who roamed through the project (the dog, not the Russian). Despite his name, people said he was an avowed pacifist. Timoshenko had belonged to a woman named Sara Dawson, but he ate all her meat rations and then deserted her to join the MPs, where apparently the rations were unlimited. Timoshenko was crazy about horses and loved to patrol the fences that surrounded Los Alamos with the MPs. He usually slept on the steps of the hospital.

I was terrified of that dog. He was big and I used to take long detours around where I thought he might be on the way to school.

On parade days Timoshenko led the way, and after him came Lieutenant Bush on his big black horse, leading the mounted MPs. The Women's Army Corps members came next—very snappy. After the WACs came the Provisional Engineers and the MPs. The Special Engineer Detachment (SEDs) were at the end of the line. They straggled along with a dejected air; every one of them out of step with the guy next to him. As a result, the SEDs were often reported for their lack of military precision. On one occasion they perfected wagging their fingers in precision, but not their steps.

WAC and chemist Helen Gowen feeds Timoshenko and friend. The buildings in the photograph with Timoshenko are the Sundt apartments. Courtesy Reid/Cameron family and Los Alamos Historical Society Archive

Chapter 9
People in and around Los Alamos

Special Engineer Detachments

The project was always short of personnel to help construct
and operate the various plants. To help that situation, on
May 22, 1943, the Commanding General of the Army
Services Forces authorized the establishment of a Special
Engineer Detachment (SED). This meant that technical
personnel could be assigned upon their induction into the
Army. In the beginning, this consisted of 334 enlisted men.
By 1945, their numbers had increased to 1,823 men. By the
end of the war about one-third of the personnel at Los
Alamos were SEDs.

Appendix 5 is an interesting first person article written
by one of the SED's at Los Alamos, Benjamin Bederson.

The SEDs were very young men, smart and very lucky
to be assigned to Los Alamos and not sent to a battlefield.
They were packed into the barracks like sardines, bunks
stacked up three high. They called themselves "The
Soldiers Different." There were no privates in the SED;
they were all corporals or sergeants.

Although most SEDs had no science education other
than perhaps a bachelor's degree, and some lacked even
that, they were plucked from the rank and file of the Army
for their technical skills and put to work solving the many
problems impeding the creation of the atomic bomb. In the
intellectual pressure cooker of the Manhattan Project, they

were an essential group. These men worked beside the Nobel laureates and other senior scientists on every problem, and many of them later went on to become scientists. They all knew they were engaged in an amazing intellectual adventure, even if they didn't know exactly what it was. It was an amazing time for all the men, but perhaps especially for the young SEDs. One SED who went on the get a PhD, MacAllister Hull, later told me, "We were all smarter than we will ever be again."

We could drive to Santa Fe but had to tell the guards at the front gate where we were going and when we expected to be back. Shopping in Santa Fe was still limited by what was available during the war, and probably was, even in the best of times, not full of merchandise. Sears and Roebucks or Montgomery Ward's catalogues were the best shopping options. At one point, apparently, Sears questioned why one address, P.O. Box 1663, needed almost 300 catalogues.

Many of the wives who were at Los Alamos during the war recalled that they had never lived in a place where people were as friendly. Laura Fermi said, "There was this kind of living, the closest I have seen in America to a communistic type of living on a somewhat large scale. We were something like 5,000 residents toward the end of the war. I haven't seen similar conditions in any other place." When she was asked about what the women talked about at Los Alamos, she said something similar to what I have heard many other women who were there say: "We talked about smuggling liquor into Los Alamos, about the road that was too steep and winding, and the WACs who drove too fast."

I don't think this is a gloss put on in retrospect. They were doing work that was extremely important. This is not to say life was perfect, but there was a strong sense of community. The problems were common problems. They all complained about General Groves. He seemed to be responsible for most of their discomforts—the balky stoves and the mud and other things—but I don't remember any complaints about security. I don't think people complained about that. It was a given, and it would not be sporting to grumble about it.

Miss Warner and Tilano

Other people who were part of the early Los Alamos community included Edith Warner—*Miss* Warner, which is how I still think of her. She lived in a small adobe house below Los Alamos where the road crossed the Rio Grande at Otowi. Los Alamos folks visited her to have a cup of tea and talk. We called the San Ildefonso man who lived with her Tilano. He had long braids and a kind, whimsical, quiet air. In retrospect I think maybe Miss Warner didn't really like children, because when our parents stopped by she usually shooed us out and said, "Go ask Tilano to take you down to the river."

Miss Warner and Tilano

Tilano. Photo credit Laura Gilpin

We would then follow Tilano down to the river. Before the Army Corp of Engineers undertook to "straighten the river out" there was a sort of marshy, long, bending meander area that had willows and birds. It was like the final resting place for the river before it plunged into the deep dark White Rock Canyon. Tilano would show us birds. Once we found a dead swan, very beautiful, which we were afraid to touch. He also showed the boys how to haft a stone axe using willow strips. Our fathers were making the atomic bomb, but we were learning how to make a stone axe. We thought it was very cool. Tilano made the axe in the photo for John Bradbury.

Stone axe made by Tilano for John Bradbury

Miss Warner seemed very important to me. This is probably because my mother and Mrs. Bradbury (later my mother-in-law) and Ethel Froman all thought she was very special. I don't think it was her tea or cooking, which was also important. Miss Warner lived in a rare harmony with the land. She loved the mesas, the sky, and the birds. She was very comfortable with the pueblo of San Ildefonso. She could walk over to it, but it seems to me that she was careful to fit in or stay out, whichever the moment decreed. She was frail but strong. I am trying to think what exactly made her special. I think it may be that somehow she shared these connections with the physicists, connections that had nothing to do with physics. She found some resonance with them: Oppenheimer, Niels Bohr, and others. It might be too much to say that the house was a refuge from the press of Los Alamos. *The House at Otowi Bridge* by Peggy Pond Church has some of her letters and is a lovely little book. It shows the sense of belonging to a place, to the land, and to that troubled time.

When Los Alamos decided they needed a better bridge, she moved across the canyon. She could not stay in her house due to traffic and noise. People from Los Alamos and the pueblo helped her build a new house and plant a new garden. She never seemed quite as happy in the new place. The pueblo of San Ildefonso used her old house as a stable for a while.

More about the Indians

As children, of course, we spoke English, but many of us wanted to learn Tewa so we could speak to the maids. General Groves thought that the scientists' wives could be secretaries to help with the important work, and so the wives would need maids. But most of the Los Alamos wives did not want to be secretaries and didn't take jobs inside the Tech Area.

Kids loved the maids, and they loved us, but we couldn't really talk to them very well. We had short lists of words in Tewa that we wanted to learn but that didn't get very far. When General Groves said he did not want the Indians to shop at the commissary which had better food, there was an immediate revolt from the wives, who said *Yes they can*, and that was that.

Some of the Indian women also worked on assembling delicate bomb parts. According to John Tucker, our neighbor at Los Alamos, "These women got real good at soldering bridge wires on the entrance plugs and loading the explosives."

We were invited to the big Indian celebrations, bought Indian pottery, and felt that they made our lives richer and more interesting. The Laboratory took over large tracts of land that were the traditional hunting grounds and location of shrines essential to the pueblos, and those losses are still felt by people today. These losses should therefore be counted in with the costs of the project.

A Strange Mix of People

What did the wives do? Mostly they used their free time to hike, ride horses, and talk. There were no telephones except in the technical areas, so if your mother wanted to talk to a friend she would just walk over and knock.

Some of the wives did work as technical assistants, doing the endless calculations on overstressed Marchant adding machines. These devices were not designed to be used as hard as they were at Los Alamos, and when they broke down they were often repaired by the talented Richard Feynman, who was assigned to the elder genius, Hans Bethe. Generally, the wives did not complain. They were well aware that other husbands and fathers were dying on the beaches of small islands in the Pacific.

Los Alamos was composed of a pretty strange mix of people including the SEDs, scientists, engineers, Military Police, maids and janitors and other workers from the

72

valley below the town. At 5,000 feet, the valley was where the muddy Rio Grande made good farmland. These workers were Indians or Hispanics who were new to a cash economy. Most were farmers. Some had homesteaded up on the waterless Los Alamos Mesa, growing pinto beans (which do not have to be irrigated). They lost their land when the Manhattan Project took over. Although the Ranch School was compensated, the farmers were not. It took many years to get the government to compensate them.

These local workers were all employed by a construction outfit called the Zia Company.. Many were farmers who lived along the Rio Grande and they held things together. They were the engine of Los Alamos. They built things, painted, worked both inside the fence and in the residential community. The influx of money from the Manhattan Project certainly changed the economy of Northern New Mexico. And without this important labor pool the project would have been impossible.

Hispanic kids went to school at Los Alamos with the rest of us. In a book called *On My Own* Dimas Chávez has written about starting first grade without knowing a word of English. I have added excerpts from this book to this manuscript as Appendix 6. But the Indian children stayed in their pueblos and went to Indian School. As kids we were aware of these differences, but that didn't mean that we were not friends. We just accepted it.

Lois Bradbury, Norris Bradbury's wife, with Isabel Atencio

Maria Martinez with physicist Enrico Fermi

It seemed to me as a child that almost everybody was interested in the Indians and helped them in every way they could. The conditions at the pueblos were hard and they certainly had not been treated well by the United States Government. They were and still are resilient, however, and have preserved their own cultures. In New Mexico in particular they found ways to endure. Each pueblo has a ceremonial calendar that is observed and sometimes outsiders are invited.

In the early years after the war the Laboratory closed on January 23, which is San Ildefonso Day, because so many of the workers at Los Alamos came from San Ildefonso. Norris Bradbury would just close the lab so the pueblo could celebrate. We all bought Indian pottery. The most prized pieces were by Maria Martinez from San Ildefonso and Desideria and Margaret Tafoya from Santa Clara. David Bradbury was learning to dance with the San Ildefonso kids, and Isabelle Atencio, the Bradbury's maid, took care of him and used to bring him down to the pueblo.

Lois Bradbury told me this story, the likes of which could have happened only in a place like Los Alamos. Sometime in the 1950s, Norris Bradbury was approached by a contingent who represented Queen Frederica of Greece to discuss a proposal to enlarge a harbor. The Queen had had a conversation with Edward Teller about using a nuclear bomb to do this. She wanted to talk with Bradbury about it.

A visit by a queen to a commoner's house was a big deal. It seems that queens won't use just any old toilet. She had a special toilet seat delivered to Bradbury's house, and it was installed in one of the bathrooms for her use in case she needed it. She also had to have a special designated chair to sit on in Bradbury's house.

Lois was extremely excited and very nervous about this pending visit. Royalty doesn't come calling just any day—in fact, prior to this day, never. She wanted everything to go perfectly. She arranged for a couple of Indian women to come and assist. The women, including Maria, the famous San Ildefonso potter, arrived before the Queen to help set everything up. The Bradbury's house had a fairly long, narrow driveway. The Indian women didn't drive, so they had their husbands drive them up from the pueblo in their pickup trucks. They, of course, parked in the driveway, completely blocking it so that Queen Frederica's limousine could not to get to the house.

Either earlier that day or the day before, Queen Frederica had visited San Ildefonso pueblo to meet the famous potters of the pueblo and see the artwork they produced. When the queen arrived, she had to get out of the limo and walk down the driveway to get to the house. She passed by the Indians, whom she had met previously and been introduced to as Queen Frederica. The Indians didn't know what a queen was, and thought that her first name was Queenie. So they all called out "Hi, Queenie, how are you doing?" Lois practically had a heart attack. But apparently the day went well, except when the Queen had a chance to speak with Norris about enlarging the harbor by exploding a nuclear bomb in it. He said sure, that could work, except you would have to evacuate most of the country and couldn't use the harbor for many years due to radioactivity.

Chapter 10
Los Alamos After the War

After the war, the first thought was to shut down Los Alamos.. It would no longer be needed. However, it soon became obvious that the Soviet Union was a threat. The Cold War with its attendant arms race and the development of the hydrogen bomb kept Los Alamos important. But primitive living conditions were no longer satisfactory for families. Better houses were built, first in the Western Area and later over the mesas. More schools and a shopping center were built. Los Alamos took on aspects of a real town. We still had passes and there were still explosions, though, so things were almost normal.

We got a house in the Western Area and had very nice neighbors. We played in the nearby canyons and walked to the new school called Mesa School.

A permanent Western Area house. Source: The Manhattan District History, Nonscientific Aspects of Los Alamos Project Y. 1942 through 1946. Written by Edith C. Truslow and edited by Kasa V. Thayer. Available from National Technical Information Service 5285 Port Royal Road, Springfield, Virginia 22151 Issued March 1973.

The Western Area featured real houses. Ours house at 1420 45th Street had three bedrooms, one bathroom, a living room, dining room, kitchen, and a one-car covered carport. It was like the house shown above, just after completion. Life for a kid was as close to perfect as one can imagine. Summer weather in the Northern New Mexico high plateau (altitude 7,500 feet) was great. We spent long days in shorts, tee shirts and no shoes, playing games, putting on plays and circuses, riding bikes, roller-skating (shoes required with clamp-on skates that always fell off), and hiking in the nearby canyons and mountains. We did all the things that we now don't let our kids (or grandkids) do—staying out all day without checking in, drinking from the hose, playing with knives, getting sunburned, falling out of trees, and in general being kids. Saturday mornings were spent riding bikes to the movie theater which showed Roy Rogers movies for ten cents. Roy was the King of the Cowboys. I remember worrying about who would be King of the Cowboys when Roy Rogers died. Hopefully not Gene Autry. I hated Gene Autry!

Our family at Christmas in the Western Area house

Winters brought snow, but not the bitter cold of much of the country. We made igloos of snow bricks that we packed in cardboard boxes. One winter our fathers built a long sled track, iced by spraying water from a hose. It is a wonder that no one was seriously hurt as we often went flying off the side. Maybe kids were more breakproof then, or maybe we are too protective now?

Marshall and I, along with our neighbor Bobby Howes, spent many days in the canyon near our house. We had a code of behavior including how to dress—canyon colors to blend in, no loud noises, moving slowly so we could avoid being detected. Our section of the canyon was the lower canyon, but the upper canyon was the domain of the dreaded Bradbury gang. This gang was headed by Jim and John Bradbury, the sons of lab Director Norris Bradbury, but I don't think I knew their "pedigree" at the time, nor would I have cared. There was essentially no class distinction in Los Alamos. There may have been within the Lab, but outside of work time it was hard to say anyone was much better off than anyone else.

A tremendous sort of melting-pot thing occurred, observed Jim Bradbury in *Children of Los Alamos* by Katrina R. Mason (page xii). "The Ulams [from Poland and France], the Fermis [from Italy], the Kistiakowskys [from Ukraine]. Their children mixing with the [Native American] Atencios and the [Spanish-American] Sandovals. Here you had this tremendous diversity in people, in nationalities and ethnic groups, in roles, yet somehow you had a bond of something happening that kept us all together." Some of the children went so far as to say, "The children felt no prejudice—none." Others disagree, noting that in some important ways Los Alamos was an unusually stratified community but by education and occupation, not ethnic origin.

Anyway, Jim and John Bradbury were several years older than we were, so we were careful not to have much direct contact with them in the canyon. When we did run into each other, fierce pinecone wars would break out, but they were usually pretty ineffectual because we wouldn't get close enough to actually hit each other. We both had forts. One of our main objectives was to find their fort and destroy it. This was dangerous because they might be in it. We did find it once and wrecked it for it was a sorry thing, consisting of some logs and branches over a gap between two large boulders.

Did we build a fort because we were afraid of atomic attack? I don't think so. Most kids build forts. Ours was a shallow cave under some boulders and tree roots. The Bradbury boys never did find our fort. I vividly remember one summer afternoon when we were in the canyon and a violent thunderstorm came up. We were huddled in our fort. Marshall was the youngest—probably six years old, and was scared and crying, and Bobby and I were stuffing our lunch—egg salad sandwiches—into his mouth to shut him up. The amazing part of this story is that Daddy found us. It must have been a weekend and he was home, but our parents had only a vague idea of where we all went when we were in the canyon. But he came to the edge of the canyon and whistled for us. We heard him and climbed up, wet muddy, scared and stuffed—at least Marshall was.

There was another time when Marshall and I got into a serious predicament. We decided to walk up above the Western Area houses and found the water tanks that supplied the housing development. These were big tanks that were in an area that was blasted out of rock to make a flat floor for the tanks. The rock walls of this area were natural climbing challenges, maybe thirty feet high. We climbed up but couldn't get down. Fear, lack of hand- and footholds, down is harder than up—for whatever reason, we were stuck. We were far enough up the Jemez Mountain that yelling for help was not working, we were just too far from the last houses. It was getting dark, past dinnertime, we were stuck, and more and more afraid. Again. Daddy found us. How he knew where to look for us, I have no idea. It took the fire department to get us down.

In Los Alamos there was no junior high school. We went from elementary to high school. I had a friend, Butch Humpherys, who was in the Radio Club and had been asked to run the projector for a conference. I am not sure, but this may have been the first conference on the effects of atomic weapons. Why did they have a high school kid run these films? I don't know. Probably because he knew how to run the projector. This was unedited footage of Hiroshima and Nagasaki with no sound or commentary. Butch said I could come up to the projection booth and hang out, so I did. We were, of course, watching the film. I was stunned, shocked.

I really thought, or hoped, that perhaps our fathers did not develop this weapon. Or that maybe they didn't know what happened after it was dropped. I wondered if they knew what was going to happen when they dropped the bomb? I began to ask some of the men, and some really took me seriously. Looking back, nobody ever told me to stop asking "Did they know what was going to happen when they dropped the bomb?" questions.

In the late 1950s Oppenheimer came back to Los Alamos as a consultant, but since he had lost his security clearance, he could not go behind the fence. This is a sad story of a vicious political and personal vendetta by Lewis Strauss. There was never any real question of Oppenheimer's loyalty to the United States, and the hearings he endured before the Atomic Energy Commission almost destroyed him. When he came back to Los Alamos he was venerated.

Norris Bradbury had a party for him. Joyce Eister, the caterer, asked several local girls to help out and pass hors d'oeuvres. She saw Oppie alone in the living room and told me to go offer him something. As I mentioned, I had been asking various physicists and people I knew what they thought about the whole project because I had seen, by accident, some of the films - people wandering in the river with their skin falling off. I was appalled.

And suddenly, at this party, there was Oppie, thin and frail but alone for a moment in the large, beautiful living room of the Bradbury home. I remember I had on a pink frilly summer dress. I was probably fourteen or fifteen years old. I really didn't think Oppie was a real person. To me he was a legend. I had no idea I was talking to a person who, as the historian Priscilla McMillan described him to me, had an immanent sense that he, who had given the world the atomic bomb, was indeed guilty of anything he was accused of.

I went up to him with a plate of chicken wings, offered him one, and said: ". . . and I think you are some kind of a saint."

Oppie looked surprised: "Why would you ever say that to me?"

"Because you had second thoughts."

He was just stricken. I could see his face change. It was like he was going to cry or something terrible was going to happen.

He turned away, took his hat from the baby grand piano, where he always left it, and walked out and did not come back. Lois Bradbury came up to me and said, "What did you say to Oppie?"

I was stricken too. The idea that anything I said would have affected him had never occurred to me. I think he was really caught unaware that the question was recognized so widely, that there was no place he was safe anymore, that

83

he had opened the Pandora's box and it was never going to close.

I hadn't intended any of that. He was the only person I could think of who had tried to figure out how complicated this was. I had thought, Well, maybe here's the man who really worried about this. I had thought maybe he and I were the only people who were worried, so I was going to tell him I thought he was a kindred soul. The idea that I had touched him really scared me.

Chapter 11
The Valley

In 1952 when I was in eighth grade, about to be a freshman in Los Alamos High School, we moved to The Valley. At the time in Los Alamos you couldn't own a home. All housing was rented from the Government. My parents wanted to own and to have some land, so they bought a house on four acres in the Espanola Valley on the Rio Grande near Black Mesa. The house was not really finished but was livable. Finishing it and taking care of the land was an unending task for Daddy and his reluctant workers: Marshall and me.

This new house had a big swimming pool. So we had pool parties. Everyone swam as fast as they could because the water was freezing. The well water came in at about 56 degrees and in a week or so it warmed up and turned green with algae because there was no filter or chlorine system like pools now have. Then Daddy pumped it out and refilled it, and again, it was very cold.

At some early point Claire Ulam, came to test a new bathing suit her father, Stan, had brought back from Paris. This was the height of Bridget Bardot's shocking exposure of her many assets. At the age of twelve or so, Claire had none of them.

But Stan, who had a great sense of humor, thought the name of the bathing suit was funny, a Bikini because like the atoll it was all blown away. (The first test of a hydrogen bomb, which Stan had figured how to detonate, was done on an atoll in the Pacific named Eniwetok, near the Bikini Atoll.)

So Claire arrived and we went into my bedroom to help her put on this tiny scrap of cloth. Shocked, we were sure this would never catch on. No woman would *ever* wear such a thing. Claire never got out of the bedroom. We agreed, no, oh my gosh, the Bikini was too revealing. Little did we know.

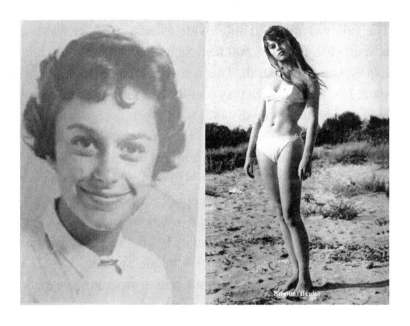

Left: Claire Ulam, age 16, photo from the Los Alamos High School yearbook.
Right: Brigitte Bardot modeling a Bikini

Thinking about this, it wasn't a loss of innocence. It was a package deal that had been made as a result of circumstances and opportunities at a critical time of war.

We knew what the bombs could do and had done. We knew that they had been invented at Los Alamos. We knew it was going to be hard, probably impossible, to undo. But I was sure of one thing, no one would ever wear a Bikini.

When we talk about The Valley, we are talking about a part of the Rio Grande Valley in Northern New Mexico. It is bounded on the west by the Jemez Mountains and the Sangre De Christo Mountains on the East. The Jemez mountains are 10,000 feet high, and the Sangre De Christos are almost 13,000 feet at the highest point in New Mexico. The valley is about 20 miles wide where our house was and is at an elevation of 5,500 feet. Santa Fe is to the south and Española is to the north. This is a very pretty part of the state. No matter which way you look in the valley there are high mountains in the distance with green evergreen trees and aspens that in the fall are a rich golden color. The air is clean and crisp, and the sky is a bright blue.

The pueblos of the various Native American peoples style heavily influence the culture of the region along with Spanish American people, some of whose ancestors came to Northern New Mexico in the early 1600s. There was not much Anglo influence north of Albuquerque until Los Alamos became home to various scientists, engineers, and their families in order to work on the bomb.

I know that my Grandmother Wilder did not want Daddy to go on working in New Mexico after the end of the war. She believed a gentleman did not work. But by then Daddy had fallen in love with the region. The work at S-Site was exciting and important, and being a gentleman was not. I think that for both our parents, New Mexico was a new and different world, and they never went back to

Kentucky except to visit family. As we settled into the Valley, we played with some of the Indian kids and wandered all over their land. We learned where the sacred pools were and that we shouldn't go there. These pools often had rattlesnakes protecting them. We went to the Indian dances at San Ildefonso and could hear the beat of the big drums from our house.

A Girl and Her Horse

Horses had been part of Los Alamos since I was little, but when I was 13, I *had* to have a horse. Girls love horses much more than boys do. So we bought Star, a big black horse with a white star on his forehead. He was an American Saddlebred and had been in rodeos as a barrel racer. Barrel racing is a rodeo event in which three empty 55-gallon oil drums are set in a triangle in a pattern like first, second, and third base in baseball, but about 100 feet apart rather baseball's spacing of 90 feet. Home plate is where the racer starts. The horse must be fast and turn on a dime.

That was Star. So I became a barrel racer. Most barrel racers are girls because they weigh less, so the horse isn't carrying as much as he would if a man were riding him. Think of a horse starting at home plate, running at 40 miles an hour to first base, going around the barrel, running to third base and around that barrel, tearing to second base and turning around that barrel, and then running at top speed back to the starting line, where he has to make an immediate stop because this is in a rodeo arena and there is a fence at the end. Very exciting for the horse, rider, and fans. Whoever does this the fastest without knocking over a barrel is the winner.

Star was an athlete, as was I. And like most human athletes, he became very excited when he knew that he would race, and he remained very excited after racing. I would practice at our house in the valley. All it took were three oil drums. One time after Star had run the barrels several times, I asked Marshall to cool Star down. That is, ride him slowly until he calmed down. Then we could put him in his horse lot and groom, feed, and water him.

Marshall was a good rider, so he saw no problem. He could just ride him around and talk to him. But Star had other ideas. He took the bit in his teeth and took off at a dead run through the neighbor's apple orchard. The tree limbs were barely high enough for him to get under them, and definitely not enough for him and a rider. Marshall did the old Indian trick of getting over alongside his neck and hung on. He had essentially no control of the horse, but finally did get him turned toward home and back into the horse lot. Mother, Daddy and I were watching all of this, probably thinking that he was dead or would soon be, but after he ran into the lot, we closed the gate. Star did a barrel racing turn at the end of the lot, ran up to the gate, and stopped. Mother asked Marshall why he hadn't just jumped off. He responded, I don't think dismounting at 40 miles an hour is a very good idea.

Star came with certain conditions. He was from San Ildefonso and the men who sold him to us said they could come visit him whenever they wanted. They could whistle and Star would trot right over to them. When I whistled, he would lift his head, look, decide it wasn't important, then go on grazing. I practiced whistling but Star was not impressed. The men from San Ildefonso also made it clear that Star was supposed to go with them when they went to dance in places where San Ildefonso had been in prehistoric times. I could go, but not get off the horse. We were a package deal, but I was not the important part of the package. The men drove their pickups to two or three places where they sang and danced to bless the old places. Star had some importance to them that I didn't understand, but we went along and were very quiet. He was a very special horse.

Ellen, Carolyn, Marshall, and Star

When I was in high school, I used to "test" potential boyfriends by having them try to ride Star. In New Mexico, everyone thought they were a cowboy, and certainly no self-respecting boy would admit that he couldn't ride. Star made short work even of decent riders. Daddy got great pleasure out of seeing them get thrown in the first one or two minutes. Horses can sense when someone isn't worthy and Star was very proud. I was Queen of the Los Alamos Rodeo and Star liked being the center of attention. He had been in rodeos before and knew a lot more about what to do than I did.

Mexico City, 1956: Ellen, Language, Culture, and Inexperience

Ellen Wilder at 16

When I was 16, I was an exchange student in Mexico. After three years of Los Alamos High School Spanish classes, I thought I was ready. I was not. It was summer, but in Mexico school was in session.

I stayed with a family named Fernandez, who were Spanish, not Mexican. Like many other Spanish intellectuals at that time they had fled to Mexico from

92

Franco's Spain in the 1930s, They told me they were communists, but White Communists, not Red. They definitely were not supporters of Stalin. They supported Trotsky, and had paid for him to come to Mexico from Norway to save him from Stalin. The father, known as Papi, was in charge of the Mexican branch of the great old Spanish Press, Aguilar.

They lived in a district known as San Angel, in a very modern house that may have been designed by the famous architect, Baragan. I would share a room with Concha, who was a little younger than me, but the house was ruled by the grandmother, Abuela Fernandez, whom they addressed using the formal *vosotras*. This was a form I had never used as I thought it was used for addressing God or the King, not a living person. She also spoke Castilian Spanish. And she always used the imperative form.

Abuela Fernandez apparently thought that I must have done something pretty bad to have been sent away by my family. A girl, at such a tender age, so easy to make a mistake. She did not ask about what I might have done, and since I hadn't done anything, and I was afraid of her, I never attempted to explain.

She looked me over and announced, "Well, you will *never* get married." I understood her, but I was afraid to ask why. She explained. "You don't have pierced ears." That was true. In high school at that time, only a few very "fast girls" had pierced ears. I could not explain this to her.

So Abuela decided, unilaterally, she could at least fix that. She got a needle and thread and made me sit in a chair. I had not been in the house for even an hour. I was apprehensive. Already things were scary. I thought I had

93

better say something, but the sentence I was constructing in my head needed to be conditional, a tense I did not know very well. That in itself was a challenge, not to mention that I was going to have to use the formal style of address. Later, when I got back to New Mexico and was explaining this to my mother, she suggested that I could have just said No.

I was planning to say, in correct Spanish, "If I had been in my own country, I would not have my ears pierced." While I was working on this complicated sentence, Abuela stuck a needle through my ear and pulled the thread through the hole. It did hurt, but more than that I was very surprised that it had happened so fast.

Obviously, my thoughts on the matter did not count. She was going to fix me up and find me a boyfriend from a good family who did not know about my dubious past, and that way she would provide a service for my family. Someday I could go back to wherever I came from with a nice husband and regain some of the lost family honor.

Concha was then allowed to take me up to the room we were to share so I could unpack. I tried to explain to Concha that I was afraid that my family would not like me to have pierced ears, or at least they should have been consulted. But she told me that when Abuela decided to do something, that was what they did. She thought it was a good sign that her grandmother had taken an interest in me. She said sometimes Abuela would not even speak to her friends when they came to visit.

The family abided by a strict order of importance. I had to figure this out so I could use the correct form of address for each one.

1. Abuela, *Vosotras*
2. Papi, *Usted*
3. Mami, *Usted*
4. Papi's brother's Spanish wife, whose husband had died recently, U*sted*

Here it gets a little cloudy. I learned that Papi's brother had been married in Spain and his Spanish wife was a regular member of the family. They did not have children. After he died, some other wives had surfaced. One appeared from somewhere in Guatemala but was not an Indian. There was a third wife, who was an Indian. They had all moved in with the Fernandez family. The Spanish wife consulted with Mami about everything. The Guatemalan wife was turned into a maid. The Indian wife did not ever come out of the kitchen, so I don't know what she did.

It was hard to judge their importance. This meant I had to figure out how I should address them. Formal, familiar, or better not at all.

5. Concha, who became my friend, *Tu*
6. They did not have a son, but two more girls, Menchu and the baby, *Tu*
7. Everyone else was easy. The maids, gardeners, and chauffeur, *Tu*
8. Concha's friends, *Tu*
9. The nuns at school, *Ud*

Concha and I went to the Universidad Motolinea. This was a Catholic girls' school where the nuns were in charge and you were not supposed to wear lipstick. But on break, some of the girls would put it on, and then wipe it off before going back to class. Some had already had their Quinceañera, which in Latin America occurs when a girl turns 15. There is a big party that introduces you to society, and you could go out with boys and wear makeup. I could, because I was already 16, but Concha had not yet had her Quinceañera.

At the house, the children ate first at meals except on important occasions. Abuela, Papi, and Mami sat down later or earlier, but not with us. The food was Spanish. We could not watch TV because the family was in mourning for the dead brother. We also had to miss seeing Cantinflas in a bullfight because we were in mourning. This mourning also affected Concha, who was not allowed to go out with friends.

Somehow Abuela found a suitable boyfriend for me: Fernando Autrique. She informed me that he was from a good family. They were French and had big sugar plantations in Cuba. He was blond, like me, had blue eyes, and, though I am not sure this figured into her calculations, a light blue Chevy Corvette convertible. This was good, but way too dangerous for me to ride with him, way too dangerous.

When Francisco and I went out, this is how things were arranged. Francisco drove his car in front alone. Then Concha and two or three maids and I followed in their car, driven by their chauffeur.

Concha was crazy about the actor Errol Flynn. We would drive to a movie house somewhere in Mexico City where there was an Errol Flynn movie, and then we would all sit in one row. I could sit next to Fernando but not touch.

He put up with all this elaborate distancing. We had only a few private conversations. On one very memorable occasion I went to a dance at the Club España. Concha could not go because she had not had her Quinceañera and her family was still in mourning.

The prospect of the dance was very exciting. Concha told me it was the most elite club, and only Spanish people could join. Papi was a member. I was invited by Fernando but would have to be escorted by at least two maids and her aunt. The club was decorated everywhere with daisies. The dance was held in a big ballroom, with chairs along all the walls. There was a band and they played waltzes and tangos and cha-cha-cha. I wore a pretty aqua-colored dress, shown in the picture above, with lilies of the valley embroidered on the skirt. I don't think I wore makeup or high heels. Fernando wore a tuxedo. I liked the dance and Fernando. When we were not dancing, I sat with the maids and the aunts, not Fernando.

There was not much opportunity to talk. Fernando had a plan, however, which involved dancing nearer and nearer to a balcony and then finally stepping out onto it so we would be alone.

And we were, at last, alone in the moonlight. He took my hand and gazed into my eyes and said *"Te quiero."*

I don't know if I said anything, but I thought: Hmm, I know that is a transitive verb that needs a direct object. I thought it was an incomplete sentence, so I waited. What does he want? He looked pained. I didn't know what to do.

The moment passed and we had to go back inside and keep on dancing.

Later when I was telling Concha, she nearly fell off the bed. *What?* What did you say? I said I didn't know what he wanted.

Dios mio. And more. She explained what he said. (I love you.)

It was much more serious than I had thought.

***

The other serious thing I learned is that my hosts, the Fernandez family, supported Leon Trotsky. (Trotsky was a leading Marxist revolutionary of the first half of the 20th century.) They had paid for Trotsky and his family to come to Mexico after being deported from Norway. With Diego Rivera's urging, Mexican President Lazaro Cardenas invited Trotsky, his wife Natalia, and his grandson Esteban to find refuge in Mexico (Esteban may have joined them later—Stalin by then had killed all Trotsky's children). The Fernandez family generally supported them, even years after the assassination of Leon Trotsky in 1940. What this meant in practical terms was that about once a week we went out to Coyoacán to the Trotsky's villa. While the adults talked—Mama and Tia, because Papi often did not go—Concha and I wandered around the garden.

This was long before the house became a museum. It was large and fortress-like. There was a bust of Trotsky on the patio and the room where the failed Siqueiros assassination attempt had taken place. We could see the bullet holes. The grandson, Esteban, and his wife and tiny baby lived in a small room near the kitchen where they sat on stacks of propaganda instead of on chairs. The furniture in the house was all covered with sheets, and we didn't sit in there. With plans to make the house into a museum, they lived in only two rooms.

Most days Esteban drove to the center of Mexico City, the Zócalo, to hand out propaganda. The Trotskys had a big red armored car that was supposed to protect Trotsky. Esteban drove it, but it got terrible gas mileage and often he would run out of gas. Then he would call Sr. Fernandez, who would send his chauffeur to get some gas, pick up the Trotskys, and take them back to Coyoacán.

As young as I was, I realized this was a kind of communism that was unusual. The Fernandez family said they were White Communists. They were very rich. They lived in an exclusive district called San Angel in a beautiful modern house on the outskirts of Mexico City. They were not Stalinist, or Red Communist. I understood that it was alright to be a Communist if you were not a *Red* Communists. Looking back, this was a bit much to unravel, and I didn't.

I wrote a postcard home to Mother and Daddy that I was visiting the Trotskys. Daddy immediately wrote saying "Don't write postcards to Los Alamos mentioning the Trotskys." The mail at Los Alamos wasn't censored anymore, but he thought it might just be better to use an envelope.

***

It became clear to me that my boyfriend Fernando's ideas of a future, including marriage, were not what I wanted. He was going to give me a fur coat, a fancy car, and so on. I told him I wanted to go to college, and he was fine with that. But probably not in the United States. A good education was possible in Mexico, but I had a feeling that a trap I hadn't seen was closing on me.

When the time came for me to return home, it was with many thanks to the Fernandez family and elaborate goodbyes from Fernando's family, who drove with us but not in the same car, that we went to the airport. Fernando's sister showed me the kind of fur coat she was wearing and said that he would probably get me an even better one. I was scared and glad when I could board the plane.

On the plane, the man sitting next to me was an American and very nervous. He offered me a drink. I said I didn't drink. He said after this flight you might think about starting. It was a pretty chaotic flight, with my seatmate, who had more experience than me with flying, muttering *Oh my god*, etc. There was a loose ironing board that kept sliding back and forth down the aisles. I thought he was not being cool at all. This was only my second flight, so I was not sure what was normal, but apparently there was really something wrong.

We had to land in Chihuahua instead of Juarez because the pilot was drunk. And then waited until they flew another pilot up from Mexico City.

It all seemed fine to me.

***

Norris Bradbury and Robert Oppenheimer in 1964 at Los Alamos

Norris became the second director of Los Alamos in 1945 after the successful bomb work ended the war. He retired in 1970. We are not going to dwell on his very successful career as a nuclear physicist, but it is interesting that in July 1945, Bradbury supervised the preparation of "the Gadget," as the bomb was known, at the Trinity nuclear test. "For me to say," Bradbury later recalled, "I had any deep emotional thoughts about Trinity . . . I didn't. I was just damned pleased that it went off." This statement is very Norris Bradbury in nature. He was a no-nonsense person. He did not like to argue, did not like small talk, and was almost always the smartest person in the room.

He had many interests, including woodworking. He built from scratch the bed that he and his wife, Lois, gave John and me for our wedding. After he retired from The Lab, he went on several extensive four-wheel drive trips to remote parts of Mexico. Our father went on at least one of these with Norris and Clark Carr, who owned the small commuter airline that serviced Los Alamos. Daddy had a four-wheel drive Ford Bronco V8 that he said greatly surpassed Clark's massive Jeep Wagoner in capability and reliability.

***

Living in the Valley

Back when we moved to The Valley, the closest family to our house were the Fromans. Darol and Ethyl Froman had two daughters, Kay and Eva. Eva and Marshall became close friends. Both were in fifth grade at Los Alamos and were at the time the only kids living in that part of the Valley, which was named Pajarito Village. The Fromans owned a fairly large amount of property along the Rio Grande. They had owned the four-plus acres that our house was on, but sold it to Harry Allen, who built the house and then sold it to my parents. Several years later they sold other pieces of property on which the new owners built houses and brought other children, including the Schriebers, whom we will discuss below.

Darol Froman had been with Enrico Fermi at the University of Chicago when they achieved the first controlled sustained chain reaction nuclear test in 1942, so he was a natural to be selected to go to Los Alamos. Darol was Los Alamos Lab's deputy director from 1951 until he retired in

1962. He worked closely with Bradbury, Edward Teller, and Stanislaw Ulam on the design of the hydrogen bomb. He was also heavily involved with Project Rover to develop a nuclear thermal rocket.

The Fromans lived in a large old adobe house that was probably built shortly after the turn of the twentieth century by a Spanish American family, when the Indians were still legally allowed to sell parts of their reservation land. Darol was very smart, and we children found him easy to talk to. I remember that he was always well dressed and wore dress shoes rather than work boots even when working on a broken pump or other endless tasks of home maintenance.

We, the Wilders, often got together for celebrations with the Fromans and the Schriebers. The Fourth of July was always a big deal. At that time in New Mexico there weren't laws about what fireworks were and were not legal. This led to some fairly major displays. Marshall was the designated fireworks expert, and somehow managed to not blow off any important body parts.

One Thanksgiving with the Fromans, before serving the turkey, Darol came armed with his usual science question or fact. This time it was an explanation of the Doppler effect. His lesson was clear and interesting. A few years later, when I was taking the Graduate Record Exam, I could only answer three or four of the questions in the math section. I had not been good at math, so I had time to read to the end of the test, which had a couple of questions about the Doppler effect. I answered those. They were multiple choice and I didn't have to do the math; I knew what the effect was. A few weeks later I got a call saying I should come to the University of New Mexico and answer a few questions, including: "How could you not remember how to multiply or divide fractions and then get the Doppler effect questions?" "Oh, that was easy," I said, "Darol Froman had explained it to me and some other kids." "Oh," they said, "those kids from Los Alamos."

Darol Froman

As teenagers living in the Valley, we went to school at Los Alamos. Every morning someone's father had to take us up the hill to school and every afternoon someone's mother had to pick us up at the grocery store when we got out about 3 or 3:30 pm. If we had an activity after school one of the fathers would pick us up and drive us back down the hill later.

Los Alamos had grown and there must have been something like a Civil Defense group that was worried about Los Alamos being targeted by the Soviets, who also had atomic bombs. I don't know if this was cleared by the Lab or not, but given the isolated location on top of a mesa, getting the whole population out of town even in the best of circumstances was not going to be quick or easy.

One day Los Alamos was having a practice evacuation in case of an atomic attack. As we all knew, this was sort of silly in a town that only had two roads in or out. There was no fast way out. Cars were lined up, backing up, and stuck. We just wanted to go home like we did every day. But we sat in this traffic jam and waited. An evacuation was futile because of the geography. That day Darol Froman, who was then the assistant director of the Lab, was our driver. He was fuming about the stupidity of trying to evacuate in the face of an atomic bomb attack. He finally turned to us: Paula Schreiber, whose father had carried the plutonium core that was the inside of the Nagasaki bomb, Marshall Wilder, Ellen Wilder, and his daughter Eva, and he said:

"I want you to promise me something."

We all said, "Okay. What"?

"That if you ever see a big bright light, you will not run away, but just walk towards it."

"Okay."

We all promised.

***

105

A photo of (seated, left to right) Norris Bradbury, Leslie
Groves, and Eric Jette as well as others looking over a map.
Colonel Lyle E. Seeman stands behind Bradbury, second
from left; Colonel E. E. Wilhoyt stands at right. Standing
third from the left is Darrel Froman. John Manley is
standing third from right.

The Fromans sold a piece of their land to Marge and
Raemer Schrieber, who built an adobe house about 500
yards from our house in the Valley. This still amazes
Marshall, who worked with him on the house: How did he
know how to build a house, with only hired help to make
the adobe bricks out of the dirt where the house was built?
He was a nuclear physicist. What does that have to do with
building an authentic old-style adobe house? It took several

years, working on weekends, but they moved in with their daughters, Paula, who was Marshall's age, and Sara.

At Los Alamos, Schreiber worked on improved reactor designs until April 1945 when he was transferred to Gadget (G) Division as a member of the pit (core) assembly team for the Trinity nuclear test. He observed the explosion from the Base Camp on July 16. Nine days later, Schreiber collected another plutonium pit, which he carried in a magnesium case. They took it to Kirtland Army Air Field where they boarded a C-54 transport plane on July 26. Two days later, they arrived on the Pacific Island of Tinian where Schreiber helped assemble the Fat Man bomb that was used in Nagasaki on August 9. Comparing it with the firebombing of Tokyo by B-29 bombers that killed 100,000 people in one night in March 1945, Schreiber noted:

> Just the fact you could do the same thing with one airplane and one bomb proved the efficiency, but it didn't change the effect very much. But the firebombing, the saturation bombing of the B-29s, was not bringing Japan to its knees, and the shock effect of one airplane being able to wipe out a city, I think, is among the factors that finally convinced the Japanese military they had to give up.

See Appendix 3 for an excellent article about this bombing. This story has never before been published. Shortly after finishing writing it, coauthor Paula Schrieber Dransfield died of breast cancer. At that time I just put it aside.

Raemer Schrieber with picture of Project Rover rocket engine

***

I grew up with Kathy Manley, and Marshall was a classmate and good friend of her sister Harriot (Kim) Manley. Their father, John Manley, was one of the first physicists recruited by Oppenheimer to go to Los Alamos. He had worked with Oppie at the University of California, Berkeley before becoming a group leader during the Manhattan Project. Throughout the war Manley served as one of Oppenheimer's principal aides, with particular responsibility for laboratory management.

John Manley

Marshall and Harriot were friends through school and college. Marshall remembers helping her father with extensive remodeling of the old adobe house that the Manleys purchased in La Masilla, near Española.

Chapter 12
Ellen Gets Married

In high school I had several boyfriends. They would
drive down to the Valley to pick me up, and then have to
take me home later, so they had to have a car. I always
liked John Bradbury, even if he threw pinecones at me
when I was in fifth grade. But I didn't go out with him. I
went with his friend, Jay Woodward. Jay was smart and
funny, and he had a Model A Ford that he drove down and
then would have to stop to work on the car before it would
start again. My father often got involved in whatever repair
they were working on, and I would wait in the house,
dressed up, but not interested in the car problems.

I skipped my senior year of high school and I went to
the University of New Mexico. I joined a sorority. I was an
art major and got into an Honors program. At some point I
realized that I *really* liked John Bradbury. He was going
from school to school and getting good grades but deciding
that whatever he was studying that year was not what he
wanted. In the summer we went out, but it didn't seem
serious to me.

I think it was my junior year, however, when I was
about to go off to the University of Vienna, that John wrote
me a very passionate letter and I thought, Hmmm, that
seems like a good idea. And when I got back from Vienna,
we told our parents we wanted to get married. Well, first
we went to Santa Fe to tell Dorothy McKibbin. John was
very close to Dottie and somehow we thought that if Dottie

thought we should get married, that was a blessing, and we proceeded.

Was I impressed that John's father, Norris, was director of the Lab? Not too much. After our announcement, Norris sort of interviewed me: What did I like to read? Did I want to have children? I had not thought about children, but immediately after we were married, I got pregnant. At this point in my life, I wanted to be an artist, to write and travel. Nothing very extraordinary there.

I was comfortable with John, and we were both interested in archeology when we were in college, though not at the same school. In 1959, John and I were married in the Episcopal church, Trinity on the Hill, and had a lovely reception at Fuller Lodge which included a number of physicists, maybe even some Nobel laureates. We invited the whole pueblo of San Ildefonso, and John invited some Hispanic guys he had worked with from the Trail Crew of Bandelier. The Trail Crew got drunk almost immediately. The Indians from San Ildefonso brought pottery to the reception which was wonderful. I got a beautiful black bowl from Maria, the famous potter from San Ildefonso.

I realized this was not quite the way most wedding guest lists were assembled, but everybody was happy.

My grandmother talking to San Ildefonso Indian Isabell
Atencio at my wedding.

Ellen and John Bradbury

After we were married, we rented a small adobe house in Old Town Albuquerque and went back to school with me pregnant. John joined the National Park Service and got a job at El Morro National Monument. He had been hired to be the monument naturalist/archeologist. El Morro was, and still is, pretty much in the middle of nowhere, south of Grants on Highway 53, which is an old stagecoach route.

The National Monument is covered with inscriptions from early Spanish expeditions scratched into a huge sandstone formation that looms over a pool of water. This was the only water source for early travelers in that area. In those very early days, travel was on horseback, so trails zigged and zagged from scarce waterhole to scarce waterhole. The Indians, the Spanish conquistadors, the first Ford car, and tourists all stopped to get a drink and sign the rock.

The road to El Morro Monument, New Mexico Highway 53, was not paved. The nearest towns, Gallup and Grants, were each more than an hour away in opposite directions. This is high, ponderosa pine forest, with occasional Navajo shepherds and, off to the west near the Arizona line, the old Indian pueblo of Zuni. There was a very small Mormon town, Ramah, settled when Pancho Villa chased some of the polygamous Mormons who had settled in Mexico back into the United States. Ramah, about twenty miles from the Monument, had a trading post, but no gas station. The only place to get gas was a little bar/gas place called Tinaja.

The town of El Morro then consisted of three buildings spaced about five miles apart. The first was Tinaja. The owner was Gus, a strange man who thought that Tuesday was a national holiday, and he would not sell gas on a national holiday. If people stopped and wanted to buy gas on Tuesday, he got his rifle and often offered to shoot them.

Sometimes people who had stopped to buy gas arrived at the Monument somewhat disturbed. They would tell the ranger that a man had tried to shoot them, and he would say: "Oh, is it Tuesday? Well then . . ."

Gus lived with a Navajo woman, so he was referred to as a "squaw man." He was not on very good terms with his neighbors who were Mormons and did not approve of alcohol or living with a Navajo woman. John and I lived in a small two-room cabin on the Monument. The Monument superintendent was usually not around because of his medical issues. The only person who lived there besides us was a part-time maintenance man who was mostly concerned with keeping track of his cows, so he wasn't always around either. There was one phone in the park office, which was a short distance from the house. This phone was a single-wire party line, often in use or blown down by the wind.

The only radio station that had any reception was in Navajo, and it mostly played rock and roll and had a swap shop. We were truly isolated. The mail came twice a week. Sometimes, if our water source, the pool, got too low, we would run out. That meant someone had to haul water from a well sixty miles away. You learned to be pretty careful about using water.

But we had records and books and were not worried. I was pregnant with my first baby, due in July. That seemed a long way away. When we moved in, we were told the most important man to know was the snowplow driver, Almy Lambson. If you really need to get out in the winter, you had to get a call through to Almy to see if he would plow the road. That is, if the phone was working. Otherwise, you were stuck.

The other part of the town of El Morro was the house of a Mormon lady, who ran a sort of post office/trading post, but it was usually not open. She had several kids and was pretty busy. Sometimes she sold eggs—if the chickens were laying.

Between the Mormon lady's house and the entrance to the Monument there was a gap of three or four miles. So the last part of town was El Morro National Monument, and we lived there. A total of three buildings, which were not very close together, constituted the whole town.

Although it appeared on maps of New Mexico, El Morro was easy to miss.

About a month after we had settled in, a tourist who stopped by told John that a big storm was due. "A big snowstorm," he told me. "That will be interesting."

That evening it was quiet, maybe too quiet, maybe there wasn't going to be much of a storm. It felt strange.

When night came, though, the temperature suddenly dropped and the wind picked up. We thought, this is it. But then the wind stopped, and it was quiet. It began to snow dense, heavy flakes in silence, almost pounding down. It was spooky, crazy, seemed to be happening too fast. The snow piled up and up, drifted, and of course closed the road.

We were the only people at the Monument. John went over to check that the heat was on in the park office and found the phone ringing. It was the State Police: "We just got a report of a shooting at the Tinaja gas station. Could somebody check it out?" They knew the road was closed, but they needed to find someone who could see what had happened.

John came back to the cabin covered with snow. He had a jeep, but even that was not going to get through. He probably could not even get out of the Monument to the main road. He didn't have a gun and was not exactly sure what authority he had as an archeologist. But he was the person who had answered the call from the State Police and guessed that made him responsible.

We went outside again and looked at the snow. It was pelting down, and there was no visibility. He went back to the office and tried to call the police back, but the line had gone dead.

So we did the only thing we could do: We crawled into bed under the warm covers and went to sleep.

The next morning, we heard Almy's snowplow on the road. We figured the police must have gotten hold of Almy Lambson, who was plowing the road, or at least part of it.

Somehow John got the jeep out to the main road and followed the snowplow over to the gas station. When John got there, Almy was leaning on the plow. He pointed at Gus, who seemed to be standing up beside the old-fashioned gas pump with a long hose on one side.

No, not really standing—his arm was looped into the hose and it was holding him up. He was dead, frozen hard, standing up by the pump.

Photo credit: Elvis Kennedy

The police had gotten a report from a traveling salesman who had brought a dead Navajo woman into Gallup. She appeared to have been shot.

The salesman reported he had been following the tracks of a big logging truck that could get through the deep snow.

He had a map that indicated a paved road and a town, El Morro. As the storm got worse, he figured he would stop and might find a motel in the town. He certainly could not turn around. He was in a sedan with no traction and had to stay in the tracks of the logging truck.

Through the thick snow he saw the light at Tinaja, the little bar and gas station. He thought he saw someone standing there. He found a man standing by the gas pump, his arm hooked into the gas hose, which was holding him up. He realized the man was dead. And then he saw a Navajo woman crawling around in the deep snow. She was sobbing and bleeding badly. He picked her up and put her in the backseat of his car. It was the only thing he could think of doing.

The next house he saw, a few miles down the road, belonged to the Mormon lady. The salesman knocked on her door and explained that he had a badly injured woman in his car. He needed help. She told him she did not want to get blood on her car upholstery, and anyway she was thinking of taking her kids into Ramah to rehearse for the Christmas pageant. The frightened salesman drove on, possibly contemplating the meaning of Christmas. He never saw the turn into El Morro Monument. He drove on through the storm following the tracks of the big lumber truck that was still breaking trail for him.

The salesman finally reached Gallup. The logging truck had broken a track all the way through the deep snow. The Navajo woman died during the drive. Terrified, when he got to Gallup, the salesman found the State Police office and filed a report. The State Police put the call through to

El Morro, but then the phone went dead and they heard nothing back.

The next day the temperature dropped even more. It got even colder. During that time, of course, the phone did not work.

A day or so later the State Police called back to the Monument. They just wanted to verify that Gus was dead, as the salesman had said. They did not offer to do anything. They had many reports of people who were lost or stranded but maybe not dead yet. They were looking for possible survivors: cowboys out looking for their cows, isolated ranchers, other strays of a hard life.

They said the dead man was clearly dead, and they didn't know what connection there was, if any, with the Navajo woman. So they didn't propose to do anything about it; they had their hands full. The State Police had notified the Navajo police about the Navajo woman and the Navajo Police took her body.

Meanwhile the Navajo police were out looking for Navajo shepherds who might have gotten stuck in the snow. The Zuni police were worried about the Zuni hunters who might have been caught in the storm. The Zunis and Navajos did not cooperate—they were ancient enemies. The State Police had their hands full with the highways, which were to the north of us, and carried much more traffic.

But the scattered local people who depended on that gas station worried about themselves and the impending lack of gas.

Eventually it warmed up some, the phone started working, the road opened, and the story began to emerge.

The police determined that the Navajo woman had not been shot, but stabbed to death with a Phillips head screwdriver, which left round holes that had appeared to be bullet wounds. Gus, who owned the gas station, had shot himself with a rifle he still had in his hand. There had been a thought that maybe this had been a double murder. But those who knew Gus assured the police that he probably stabbed her, and then shot himself. So there was no case to prosecute.

The local discussion, however, focused on what to do about Gus. He had died with his arm frozen in the hose of the gas pump. Since this was the only gas pump for miles around, the men had to decide if they should cut the hose to the gas tank to get the body down or cut off Gus's arm and save the hose to the gas pump. They decided to cut off his arm. They needed the gas.

The remote situation at El Morro might have brought everyone together, especially since their only source of gas was possibly gone. But the old tribal divisions held. This was about as close as they had possibly ever come to cooperating. We realized that for the Indians the death of a white man was not something that concerned them. They searched for members of their tribe. The Zunis looked for Zunis. The Navajos, who had many shepherds lost in the storm, were trying to find lost Navajos. The Mormons had the snowplow and none of them were lost in the storm. They were worried about getting gas. The staff at the Monument were a totally other group, not a part of any of these other rather tight-knit circles. The thing that brought them together was they all needed gas. So to cut the dead man's arm off was logical and was not debated. They got out a saw, not an electric saw, just a saw.

Although John and I had grown up with the Tewa people from San Ildefonso and Santa Clara, we were such outsiders that we didn't count. Nobody asked what we thought. I think that our early lives with people totally different from ourselves made this odd circumstance more acceptable. I was more shocked than John. But I certainly didn't say anything. It was their deal. The Navajo police, like many Navajo, were scared of death and they didn't want to help with sawing his arm off, but they did not object.

His body was frozen stiff and fell over. I heard that they put him in an old chicken coop, boarded it up and he stayed frozen until the ground thawed, and they could bury him.

I wondered if this was how life was going to be.

Living in isolation in 1960 at a remote National Monument was perhaps a good time to think. I was removed from all the things that usually are a part of life—new books, telephones, records, friends, even mail, which only came once or twice a week. I had to learn to bake bread because we were so far from a grocery and only had a tiny freezer. If I took a walk on the road, a kindly Baptist minister (I think he was a Baptist) would follow me trying to convert me. The Navajos were not good prospects for conversion, and I was all that was left. So to avoid him, since he did not get out of his car, I would cut across the pinon- and juniper-covered slopes, or climb up to the top of El Morro, where the road did not go. The Mormon ladies were not going to be friends. Somehow the cultural differences were too great to reach out to them, but if I had needed to, I think I would have. Sometimes we bought groceries for the Zuni Fire Lookout, who had a Shalako house and cooked all summer. She had many kids and would stop by sometimes, but not very often.

I didn't feel that this life was hard. I was interested in El Morro. I think somehow I had learned that you just figure out what you can do, and you do it. This might be something that we learned as kids at Los Alamos . . . certainly we did not belong to a culture where you complained.

When John got a job overseeing the salvage archeology for the pueblo of Zuni I could ride into Zuni and sit in the truck and watch the excavation. A very sad thing happened at the end of this dig. John had collected about ten or twelve large, beautiful Zuni pots. He called in the Zuni Tribal Council to turn the pots over to them, and the leader took a shovel and broke all the pots into little pieces. They were Zuni pots, and the Zunis did what was the right thing for Zuni.

That year we went to a Shalako dance, when the great Zuni bird gods come to visit the pueblo and to bless the new houses. (Shalako is an elaborate Pueblo Indian ceremony which marks the winter solstice. It is held in the pueblo of Zuni and in some of the Hopi pueblos. The gods come down from their homes on top of the mesas to dance to bless each new house. The Shalako are about ten feet tall and have bird-like features. All the other gods in the pueblo pantheon come to attend them and dance. They visit all the new houses to bless them, feast and admire the rich hanging textiles, turquoise and evidence of the

123

prosperous Zuni and Hopi people. Sometimes visitors are allowed to watch the ceremonies if they keep a respective distance.)

Shaliko Dancers.
This is a drawing of the dancers. Photographs were not allowed.
Mary Wright Gill 1900. Bureau of the American Ethnology 23rd Annual Report Plate LXV

Shalako is usually after Thanksgiving. It was very cold outside, but very hot in the houses where they were dancing. In those days, nobody had special gear or extra warm coats. I had a "swing" coat, grey tweed with a red lining—very fashionable, but not very warm. I was in a Shalako house, which was hot from people, cooking, and dancing, and felt I might faint. I went outside to cool off, where I did faint, and fell face first into a mud puddle. When I came to, two Navajos were trying to pour a strawberry cream soda down my throat. I couldn't figure out where I was, and I don't like strawberry cream soda, but I understood that these men were trying to help me. They only spoke Navajo and were asking me questions, probably, where is your husband? But I fainted again.

At some point John appeared and was surprised to see what was going on. I just wanted to go home and get warm. It was nothing that couldn't be remedied with a hot bath and sleep.

The established order of that time was the man worked and the woman took care of him and had children. This wasn't a bad idea, I just wanted to do more.

I did not want to go back to Los Alamos to have our baby. I asked about the hospitals in the two nearest towns, Gallup and Grants. There was an Indian hospital in Gallup, but I wasn't an Indian, and the hospital in Grants was connected to a uranium mine but served Acoma and nearby little towns. Los Alamos was a few hours away, and Albuquerque was closer, but I thought it could not be very complicated, and decided to have the baby in Grants.

To say that I had almost no idea of what I was doing is a vast understatement. When I went into labor, the phone wasn't working, so we started into Grants without calling the doctor. It was about an hour away. The Baptist minister overheard our attempted call on the party line—and decided to follow us in case something happened on the way into Grants. This was very kind of him, but John was much more worried about having to spend time praying with the Baptist minister than with how I was doing. When we got to the clinic, John disappeared and I was left with the minister, who answered the clinic's questions since the staff thought he was my husband. The last question on the form was: if the baby is a boy do you want circumcision? I didn't know what that was, so I asked the nurse. She said ask your husband, who she assumed was the Baptist Minister. He listened to the conversation and took the opportunity to flee. I figured I should say yes. When John reappeared, he thought it was hilarious. At that point, I just wanted to sit down. After a few hours of labor, the doctor came and said he was going out to the uranium mine and gave me a shot to stop labor.

The next morning I had a baby boy. He was long and skinny and bald. The only other baby in the nursery was from Acoma. He had lots of black hair and was chubby. His mother had died from appendicitis. Some people from Acoma came to see the baby. Nobody had any trouble deciding who was who.

Chapter 13
Final Thoughts—and Questions

Did growing up at Los Alamos make us special?

Another way to ask this question might be, Did we feel special? As we wrote this story and discussed the narrative with others, we were often asked if, having grown up in Los Alamos, New Mexico, we felt special. For sure, Los Alamos was different. During most of our grade school years and into the junior high school years, the entire town of Los Alamos was a closed city. There was a barbed wire topped fence around the entire town. There were only two entrances and exits from the town; these gates were each controlled by a group of Military Police, later replaced by security guards. All armed and vigilant. One had to have a pass, which had to be shown when entering or leaving the town.

Other places in the United States were and are guarded like this. Military bases are one example, but I don't know that military bases have as many residents as did Los Alamos. And unlike the children of military men and women, our parents were not in the military. They were civilians who happened to be working on top-secret atomic weapons development. Did that make us kids special? I did not think so, at least not at the time.

Who *did* think we were special were the kids in the surrounding communities, especially Española and Santa Fe. These were the only moderate-sized towns within 100 miles of Los Alamos. Santa Fe High School was the main sports rival of Los Alamos High. Football games, and especially basketball games, were a big deal between Santa Fe High and Los Alamos High, especially when the game was in Santa Fe. Come to think of it, I don't think the games in Los Alamos were as contentious as those held in Santa Fe. There were very few Santa Fe students there. They wouldn't come into the town.

I (Marshall) remember going to pregame pep rallies in the basketball gym at Los Alamos High. Cheerleaders, fight songs, cowbells, and school spirit were in abundance. Then many of the students would ride in a convoy of school buses to Santa Fe to take in a game. The games were hard fought, with much trash talking, and no matter who won there were hard feelings when the game was over. Then we were supposed to get back into the buses to return to Los Alamos. Often small fights broke out, but I don't remember any of them turning into a West Side Story rumble. As our buses pulled out of the parking lot, more than a few of the Santa Fe boys shadowed us in their cars and followed us up the road to Los Alamos, calling us names, flipping the bird, and in general being rude. Needless to say, we were doing the same thing out of the bus windows.

But as we got to Los Alamos, where the main gate used to be, they stopped—they would not go into the town. There was no barrier, fence, gate, or wall, except the one in their minds. They certainly thought there was something special about the place, and by transference there was something special about us Los Alamos kids.

But maybe we really were special. I expect that the average IQ of our parents was significantly higher than the IQ of the general population of the nation. Genetics count. But did it really matter? I don't think so, other than I expect that a greater-than-average percentage of Los Alamos kids went to college and were successful in life.

After I left Los Alamos and earned degrees in electrical engineering from the University of New Mexico and Santa Clara University, no one cared that I was from Los Alamos, if they even knew or asked. Not special at all, other than that Ellen and I can write about being from Los Alamos.

What happened to Oppenheimer after he lost his clearance?

When Robert Oppenheimer lost his clearance, it must have cut his heart out. Although it wasn't clear to me as a child exactly what had happened, I (Ellen) sort of gathered that the testimony at the hearings and support of scientists were overridden by petty jealousy. What was clear to me, though, even as a kid, was that Edward Teller had betrayed our hero, Oppenheimer. I knew men were flying back and forth to Washington to testify and explain and defend Oppenheimer, and that things were not going well at all. I also remember that the Los Alamos Library stopped getting *Time* magazine after Teller appeared on the cover. There are many accounts of these unfortunate committee meetings. Oppenheimer must have gone over and over things, but in the end was not effective in his own defense. And even if he had been, the FBI had bugged his phone, so his conversations with his lawyer were known to the FBI lawyers. To have his country turn against him must have been incredibly painful. Someone said that Oppenheimer loved his country more than his country loved him.

In 1954 Teller said something true, not exactly related to the ambiguous testimony he gave before the committee, but with an eye to clearing his name after we learned that he had essentially put the nail in Oppenheimer's coffin: "The important thing in any science is to do the things that can be done. Scientists naturally have a right and a duty to have opinions. But their science gives them no special insight into public affairs" (Richard Rhodes, *The Making of the Atomic Bomb*, 1995, p. 770).

But Teller never wiggled off the hook—that hook was sunk in deep. He was one of the historical inspirations for the title character of *Dr. Strangelove*, Stanley Kubrick's 1964 film starring Peter Sellers. Many years later, Teller called me to "straighten me out." I was amazed that such an important man wanted to talk to me. I had been running a series of programs, with the Smithsonian and several universities to look at parts of the Manhattan Project. He came over to the house and talked on various topics for about three hours. He gave me papers that had nothing to do with Oppenheimer's loss of clearance. I thought this would have something to do with his testimony at the Oppenheimer hearings, but although I looked for it, I didn't find anything relevant. Teller drank strong coffee until I ran out of sugar. He then said that he had to leave. He did not run out of things to say, but clearly, he had been cut to the quick at how the whole world of physics had turned against him.

Was the Atomic Bomb necessary to end World War II?

So, the conclusion: What did we learn?

There is no simple or clear answer, and we are not trying to sum it all up or make things tidy. Certainly, both the United States and Japan knew that Japan had lost the war, but Japan had not surrendered. Decision-making in war time, even when it was clear that the United States was going to win, was muddled, political, and opened what we might call a Pandora's Box. Once the Trinity Test proved that the explosive detonators of the plutonium device would work, there was little doubt that the weapon would be used.

Perhaps the only man who could have stopped the atomic bomb drops was President Harry S. Truman, who had only been president since April of 1945. He relied on his military personnel, many of whom did not think the new weapon, if they knew about it, would work, and were opting for an invasion. And what about the American mothers whose sons would have been slaughtered in an invasion of Japan, only to learn in retrospect that their deaths could have been avoided by using the atomic option?

How could these known and unknown consequences be evaluated, and to what avail? The more we know about the particulars of history, the faster the easy answers fade away. The Manhattan Project almost always had more money than time. The technical work done there shaped the course of modern science, which isn't given to too much abstract thinking.

We know that the atomic bomb saved the lives of many American boys who would have landed in an invasion of the Japanese mainland. We also know that most of the plutonium in the world was blown up in the Trinity Test on July 16, 1945, and in the explosion of the plutonium bomb that was dropped on Nagasaki. Another plutonium weapon probably would not have been available until September 1945. And the technology of a demonstration test to convince the Japanese to give up was so uncertain that the senior scientists who devised the plutonium bomb that was dropped on Nagasaki were only about seventy percent certain that it would work—a good reason to drop it as the second atomic bomb, rather than running a test with it. What if it was a dud?

We can't look into the future, and this look into the past isn't intended to provide answers. We have told personal stories about the people who worked in a climate of urgency, danger, and excitement. It seems to us that is an important and rare opportunity to learn firsthand about the personalities and talents that worked inside Los Alamos and the Manhattan Project. As Richard Rhodes observed, "Working against the clock to build weapons that might end a long and bloody war strained life at Los Alamos but also heightened it" (*The Making of the Atomic Bomb*, p. 564).

What do we know from Daddy? He was in the small group of men who, in early June, put the component parts together at V-Site to make sure they fit. Was this a moment of elation and relief, a moment to cowboy on top of the bomb, as in the photo of Daddy in Chapter 6. Daddy didn't talk about it. We know Oppenheimer hoped and prayed that it would be so horrible that nobody would ever use such weapons again. And well into the twenty-first century they have not been used. What is also true is that once it was clear how to do it, almost everybody wanted a bomb:

Mutually Assured Deterrence. And that game had bigger stakes.

From the beginning, there were attempts to restrict the use of nuclear weapons on cities, women, and children. But war is so untidy and imprecise, and the Nagasaki bomb made it very clear that isn't possible. Did Fate trick us by pushing us immediately into making a bigger, but maybe not better, bomb? Whatever the case, that is what happened. When Oppenheimer left Los Alamos in September 1945 and handed over the job of closing the Lab to Norris Bradbury, he knew that the world would never be the same. Maybe he thought a world without nuclear weapons was a luxury that would never be available again. And that has proved to be true.

Much later, Marshall asked Daddy if he had any second thoughts about his work developing the bomb. He replied emphatically, "*No!* First of all, the bombs dropped on Japan stopped the war and saved hundreds of thousands of American soldiers' lives. But maybe more importantly, the threat of nuclear war has prevented any major wars in the world for fifty years"—now going on eighty years. (This was the standard answer to a very complicated question.)

As we said in the beginning, the genie won't go back in the bottle. But we have the responsibility to understand how it got out and what we can do to prevent its use.

Looking back now, and writing about it, what seems to stand out is how much, as kids, we were influenced by the Indians. The scientists were, of course, removed from our daily life. The MPs were around and nice, never scary, just bored 18- or 19-year-old boys. They gave us rides in their jeeps and sometimes bought us ice cream.

It was the Indians who had the greatest influence on us. They lived in a very different world. Theirs had boundaries, and songs, and dances - a whole different way of living. Today there are questions about taking their sacred places away and other injustices, which was often inadvertent, and often thoughtless. Today's questions about choices, about safety, cultural differences, and effects of radiation, are not the same as those of 1943. The inclusion of the Indians in the Manhattan Project was an accident of time and place. The local Hispanic farmers were displaced from the townsite. Some of them were employed by the Project; their kids went to school with us and we were friends or not friends, just like kids are. The Indian kids went to their own schools.

Their pueblos were in the valley, not on top of the mesa, but being the nearest population, they were swept into the project sort of willy-nilly. Some of the Indian women were maids, whether or not they knew about vacuums or washing machines. We had a maid, a young woman. She was from Santa Clara Pueblo, very sweet, and pregnant. When she had her baby, alone, at home, Mother took me down to visit her, bringing some baby things and to make sure she was alright. She lived in a small adobe house in the pueblo and was sitting in a bed on the floor holding her tiny baby. I remember the small dark adobe room. She was glad to see Mother and show off her baby. It was a while before she came back to work, and sometimes she brought her baby.

Years later, when John F Kennedy was shot, I heard the news on the car radio. I drove over to Bradbury's house. Isabell Atencio, their maid, was there. I said "I want to turn on the TV." She said "we weren't supposed to", but we did. We stood together, watching as the car pulled up to the hospital in Dallas, and Jackie got out with blood all over her suit. "Just like the white man, they shoot the women too." she said. I have never forgotten that.

The Manhattan Project swept all kinds of people together without much thought about how we would get along. By and large people did get along. The people from the nearby pueblos of San Ildefonso and Santa Clara and sometime Tesuque came up to Los Alamos to work and we were invited to the pueblos to see their dances. There was a mix of people who just got along, regardless of the stress of the project, which was relentless, and certainly helped by the beauty of Northern New Mexico. For me it was the Indians who made the strongest lasting impression.

The Authors, Ellen and Marshall

Appendix 1
Description of the work done at S-Site
By Edward Wilder

I was assigned to Group X3 under Major Jerome (Jerry) O. Ackerman. Our responsibility was to develop and manufacture the high explosive system for the implosion bomb. Nobody had ever done anything like this before.

This was done at S-Site. It was on the south side as far away as possible from the rest of the Project. We believed that this was because of the danger involved in what we were doing. The personnel at S-site were almost completely military. We also believed that this was because the work was too dangerous for civilians.

We worked a nominal 8 to 5 shift, but in practice everyone worked much more than this. The plant worked a 24 hr day, six days a week. The product in the early days of the Project was used to study materials under conditions of high pressure and shock, as well as to develop the explosive lens that would implode the nuclear components of the bomb. The operation consisted of melting the high explosive (HE) and pouring it into molds whose shape was determined by theoretical calculations.

The men who conceived the idea of using explosives to implode the bomb underestimated the difficulty of doing this. As a result, the first facilities built were completely inadequate. This is no adverse reflection on these men, who were the foremost men in this field. Rather, it is an indication of the trouble that can be encountered in applying a familiar product to a new use. I do not know whether the planners of S-site anticipated continuous planning and construction of new buildings until just before Trinity day.

Notably absent from the first S-site buildings was anywhere machining could be done. The first HE castings were worked with hand tools, saws, rasps, and planes, to a template. This was done on boxes and makeshift stands on the floor of building TA-16-26. One of my first memories I have of S-Site is that of a man sawing a big piece on High Explosive on a Comp. B box. He had his knee on it just as if it were a block of wood. His left hand held a hose and directed a stream of water onto the saw which he held in his right hand. I believe that explosives other than Comp. B and TNT were processed before I arrived. I do not remember working with anything but Comp. B, TNT, and Baratol. Also, it seems that we were making more full-scale castings than scale models.

The kettles used in Building 42 were commercial stainless-steel kettles originally intended to make hard candy. They were jacketed and steam heated. The agitator was driven by an air motor.

Candy cooker used for melting high explosives. A wildfire swept through the site in May 2000, burning most of the remaining buildings. This kettle is all that remained from the area. Source: LANL

The molten explosive was poured from the kettle into a rubber bucket and from the bucket into the molds. The molds were steel weldments of the shape desired, a pentagon or hexagon. Small diameter tubes were fastened to the inside of the steel for circulation of tempering water. The mold was finished with Creator, a low melting casting alloy, around a master shape supported in the steel weldment. This Cerrotru covered the tempering coils and produced the mold that was used in producing the explosive shapes. The mold had no inner or outer radius surface. The inner radius was produced by an insert, called a toadstool. The outer radius was produced by a surface attached to the mold cover. If the piece being made was of

Comp. B, the outer surface was spherical; if it was Baratol, the outer surface was shaped accordingly.

In Building 42 we made the first effort to control the cooling patterns of the explosives as they solidified in the molds, by the use of steam heat on the body of the mold. Another device for improving the casting quality by reducing segregation was to use an air-motor-driven stirrer in the casting during the cooling cycle. One of the duties of the casting room attendants was to raise these stirrers as the material solidified.

Here we should acknowledge the debt that development of the bomb owes to self-adhesive tape. In my opinion, development of the explosive component of the bomb was greatly facilitated by the use of sticky tape. It seemed that it was used almost everywhere. I believe that a Navy junior officer named Glenn Greening spent most of his time working with Minnesota Mining & Manufacturing Company (3M) in developing tapes for different purposes.

r photo shows the temporary polar

Tape on "Gadget" Photo source LANL

It was in Building 42 that I saw a very dramatic demonstration of the inherent safety of the explosives we were processing. In the process we were using at the time, it was essential that the mold and riser unit be partially disassembled before complete solidification. Otherwise, there was no easy way to take them apart. On this day a mold and riser had solidified, and one of the operators was using a bronze screwdriver and a rawhide mallet to strip the HE away so that the riser could be removed. This was standard procedure, but on this day for some unknown reason there was an explosion under the screwdriver. It was a small explosion involving only one crystal and did not propagate to the rest of the explosive.

After casting, the HE was taken by hand truck to building 43 to be machined. The equipment consisted of one K&T milling machine located in a barricade corner.

The other machines were wood working type Delta drill presses. On liners and inner charges, the risers were machined off by using fly cutters, but the blades had a long spiral shape. Baratol was initially machined dry. The reason given was that water would dissolve the barium nitrate. It was only after I put a piece of Baratol in a sink and let water drip on it over night to prove that this was not important, that Baratol was machined wet.

The first machinist at S-site was Ernest Richie. He was a little man who weighed about 110 pounds. I remember his lifting and machining full-scale lenses that weighed about 125 pounds.

All explosive operations produced great quantities of scrap. This was collected daily and burned in an area where the east end of Building TA-16-260 is now. For the burn, the material was spread out in a single layer. Big pieces (125 pounds) were broken up into several smaller ones by hitting them with a heavy rubber mallet. These blows had to be very hard, and one man who did this was fat and always short of breath. Once, as he was breaking up some HE, a piece flew into his mouth and he swallowed it. We did not know how this would affect him, but apparently he suffered no ill effects.

Several times the explosive detonated instead of burning. The man in charge of the burning ground, and who ignited the HE, could speak clearly under normal conditions, but when he was excited he stuttered. Once when the burning ground exploded with a terrific bang, I hurried there to see if anyone was hurt. I met him driving away from the burning ground. He stopped me and said,

"Everything is all right, the burning ground just blew up." But it took about three minutes to say it.

Another time as we were spreading some cordite on the ground to burn it, it caught fire. I had always heard that a man in real danger will act impulsively to save himself, and this is what we did. Every man ran in the direction he was facing when the fire started. Some ran faster than others. I only ran a short distance and threw myself into a ditch, completely ignoring the stickers and tumbleweeds.

About this time, we began to have real trouble in manufacturing full scale lenses. Baratol components as made, inspected, and accepted would not, when put into a mold for overcasting, fit the mold. I remember working many nights trying to find out what was happening to our process. We finally realized that the Baratol was changing dimensions. This is known and understood now. Then it was new, but we were able to develop enough of an understanding to produce acceptable lenses.

The lens and inner charges were large and heavy, and the explosive material was rather fragile. We used three methods to protect the HE from chipping. The finished casting was sprayed with the best "Bar Top" varnish available, a thin layer of felt was glued to one of two mating spherical surfaces, and blotting paper was glued to the sides.

In these times there was no safety organization. After VJ Day, various safety men appeared, but they were uncertain and unknowledgeable, and accomplished little. The first real safety man at Los Alamos, in my opinion, was Roy Reider.

As things developed and it looked as if a bomb would really be built, the practice assembly of the HE components was started. This was first done in Gamma building in the main Tech area. As I said above, we were not bothered by any Safety people. The assemblies were made on a floor area padded with wrestling mats. Sometimes the pieces did not fit very well. I remember someone hitting a piece of HE that was out of line, as hard as he could with a heavy rubber mallet.

The Trinity bomb was assembled in building 516. At the end of the day, when the HE components were all put together, I thought that it should be guarded during the night. It was with great difficulty that I convinced people that this should be done

Appendix 2

"The last human will see what we saw."
Trinity – A Reminiscence
George B. Kistiakowsky
Reprinted from The Bulletin of the Atomic Scientists
Volume 36, 1980 – Issue 6

George B. Kistiakowsky

Badge photo of George B. Kistiakowsky. Courtesy Los
Alamos National Labs (LANL)

The emotional climax of wartime Los Alamos was the
Trinity test of the plutonium bomb on July 16, 1945. Most
of the staff was involved: The experimental and the
theoretical physics divisions estimated how much
plutonium to use, so that the bomb would not explode

prematurely, that is, until the enormous pressure regenerated by the implosion wave of the chemical explosive so compressed it that it would become supercritical. These divisions also deduced that before this compression was succeeded by expansion, huge quantities of energy would be released by the rapidly proliferating nuclear chain reaction; naturally, it had to be started at the right instant.

The chemical-metallurgical division reduced the material received from the Hanford plant into metallic plutonium, fabricating it into two hemispheres with a central cavity, a difficult process because of that metal's odd properties. The G division made the critical assembly experiments to confirm calculations on how much plutonium to use; it built the metallic "pit" of the bomb, concentric with plutonium, as well as the initiator at its very center that would release a burst of neutrons when struck by the pressure wave.

Another division, designated X, developed the spherical implosion charge, an assembly of segments cast from slurries of explosives. It was so designed that detonations started simultaneously at certain points on the surface of the charge would be converted by its explosive lenses into an implosion, that is, into a convergent detonation wave propagating toward the plutonium sphere at the center. The X division and the G division also developed novel electric detonators having unprecedented timing accuracy, and an electronic gadget called the X unit, so designed as to fire simultaneously several of the new detonators. Only the ordnance division, which was to convert our experimental device, code-named the Gadget, into an aircraft bomb-with its proximity fuses, aerodynamic outer shell, etc.-was not directly involved; but it was very active in building the other bomb, which utilized fissionable uranium. Ordnance was also preparing for the military uses of both bombs.

The real difficulty with the implosion bomb project was that at the start there were no known experimental methods to determine how perfect-and, if not, then why not-were the implosions of smaller experimental charges that were fired in many configurations and observed by a variety of methods invented in the X and the G divisions. These took place at about a dozen sites scattered over the mesas, mostly miles away from the Los Alamos housing center.

In the winter and spring of 1945 we were consuming daily something like a ton of high performance explosives, made into dozens of experimental charges. Evidence was thus gradually accumulating that explosive lenses were needed to achieve an implosion, but the proof of its quality remained inconclusive. Therefore, we repeatedly urged General Leslie R. Groves on his inspection visits to Los Alamos to allow us to carry out a final test implosion, with plutonium inserted, before using an identically constructed bomb militarily. Reluctantly, because plutonium was in such short supply, General Groves eventually gave permission.

The Alamogordo site chosen for the Trinity test is in the White Sands military reservation, about 200 miles south of Los Alamos, in the middle of an arid, sandy desert appropriately called Jornada def Muerto by the seventeenth-century Spaniards. Kenneth Bainbridge was in charge of selecting, and then developing, the test site. His organization grew large because, while confidence in the implosion process was growing slowly, ever more experiments were being invented and designed to observe the progress and consequences of the nuclear reaction or its absence, and the causes thereof.

Bainbridge had his field headquarters at an abandoned ranch, really just a group of crude shacks, about ten miles from the Trinity ground zero. To these he added more buildings, almost equally uncomfortable, since General Groves would not allow any "luxuries," as he defined them. Life at the Trinity site was primitive and there was grumbling by those who had to spend weeks on end here and who, because of the strictures of secrecy, could not visit nearby towns for relaxation. Nonetheless, by a near miracle of hard work, an elaborate field-test installation was created in just a few months' time.

I visited the site a couple of years ago and found most of the old structures gone. An ugly monument had been erected at ground zero, with a bronze plaque announcing, in large letters, that a certain (unnamed) army general had ordered it built. The green molten sand was all gone but the desert for miles around was covered with a spiderweb of electric cables that had survived these 30-odd years in the desert climate.

As the authorities in Washington learned of the impending Trinity test they conceived of political applications for it and instructed us to carry it out before the end of the Potsdam summit conference. This deadline meant even more frantic activity at Los Alamos, especially in the X division. Among other problems, we were short of explosive castings to make the charge for the test.

The implosion charge, which weighed a few tons, was assembled from nearly 100 accurately dimensioned castings, fitting tightly together to form a sphere. These and various smaller experimental castings were made from molten slurries and were difficult to produce without blemishes although we resorted to elaborate procedures. Most troublesome were the air cavities in the interior of the larger castings, which we detected by x-ray inspection techniques but could not repair. More rejects than acceptable castings were usually our unfortunate lot.

The S-site, where all the charges were fabricated, grew into a real factory with a staff of over 200 and was my biggest headache because it could not satisfy the flood of orders from all the user groups in X and G divisions for good experimental charges and, at the same time, advance the art of high quality casting of the larger charges needed for the bomb. The squabbles over who gets what began to involve me and Bob Bacher, the G division leader, and then Robert Oppenheimer, who presided over the "Cowpuncher" Committee which was allocating priorities in the laboratory. Most of the people outside the X division had never cast explosives and it seemed impossible to convince them of the seriousness of our technical problems. To add to our troubles, a short time before Trinity Oppenheimer decided, over my objections, to go ahead with a certain test by the G division, requiring a complete duplicate set of full-sized castings. They planned to explode at Los Alamos a "Chinese" copy (that is, minus only the plutonium) of the Trinity charge in their experimental installation, designed for a "magnetic observation" method. It was to provide definitive information on the degree of imperfection of the implosion wave in the Trinity Gadget.

Well, we just did not have on hand enough fault-free castings to assemble two spherical charges and the casting of enough more would take too long to meet Washington's deadline. The problem was beyond our control because additional casting equipment on order had not been delivered in time to Los Alamos. But many tests had taught us that air cavities distorted the propagation of a detonation wave and had to be avoided at all costs. In some desperation, I got hold of a dental drill and, not wishing to ask others to do an untried job, spent most of one night, the week before the Trinity test, drilling holes in some faulty castings so as to reach the air cavities indicated on our x-ray inspection films. That done, I filled the cavities by pouring molten explosive slurry into them, and thus made the castings acceptable. Overnight, enough castings were added to our stores by my labors to make more than two spheres. After they were reinspected, Norris Bradbury, with a few of our G.I.s, did the assembling-all in all quite an elaborate operation.

To get to the Trinity site the Gadget had to be trucked through Santa Fe and Albuquerque. This was the cause of much anguish in Los Alamos because some of our influential leaders thought that our explosive assemblies were far more dangerous to handle than were ordinary aircraft bombs-which they decidedly were not. I remember climbing on the truck which had been loaded with the Gadget, and driving it for a while on Los Alamos dirt roads; these were certainly as bumpy as the roads we would encounter on the trip to the test site. Of course, as I expected, nothing untoward happened. And so, by choice, a few minutes past midnight on Friday the 13th, accompanied by Bradbury, I took the Gadget convoy to the Trinity test site.

Donald Hornig, a member of a team working on the design of the X unit, took a few of these units to Trinity several days before the test., because a number of observational instruments were to be triggered by the discharge of the X unit to assure simultaneity with the explosion. A day or two after his arrival there was a violent thunderstorm, and the X unit, by then sitting on the top of the bomb tower and being used in instrumental trials, fired spontaneously. A human storm followed, this one over Hornig's head for what appeared incompetent and dangerous design. The concern, of course, was that the same event could happen after the X unit was wired to the bomb. The vocal unpleasantness went on until Hornig discovered that the grounding wire of the X unit had been inadvertently pulled off, so that the unit probably got a huge static charge from the lightnings.

Our convoy arrived Friday morning, to encounter another emotional upheaval. Another X unit installed for the instrumental trials failed dismally the evening before and Horning spent most of the night being questioned by the senior staff. Naturally, as soon as we arrived I was told what they thought of me as the irresponsible leader trusting incompetent youngsters of the X division. Finally Hornig and I took apart the failed X unit after getting it from the bomb tower. We discovered that the teams using it to test their instruments, had greatly overworked it. The X gadget was designed to be used only once, and after assembly each unit was tested only a few times to make sure that everything worked. But the Trinity teams has used it hundreds of times in rapid succession and, as I recall the electronic switch finally burned out.

This discovery relaxed the atmosphere at headquarters for a while, but on Saturday morning the big disaster was upon us. A telephone message came from Los Alamos that the G division's "magnetic method" group found their charge's implosion so faulty that they anticipated the failure of the bomb at Trinity. Everybody at headquarters became terribly upset and focused on my presumed guilt. Oppenheimer General Groves, Vannevar Bush – all had much to say about that incompetent wretch who forever after would be known to the world as the cause of the tragic failure of the Manhattan Project. Jim Conant a close personal friend, had me on the carpet it seemed for hours, coldly quizzing about the causes of the impending failure.

Sometime later that day Bachler and I were walking in the desert and as I timidly questioned the results of the magnetic test Bob accused me of challenging no less than Maxwell's equations themselves! At another point Oppenheimer became so emotional that I offered him a month's salary against ten dollars that our imposition charge would work.

(Quite some time after Trinity, when we both were back at Los Alamos, - he gave me, at a large meeting, an autographed ten dollar bill and did it ceremoniously.)

Sunday morning another phone call came from Los Alamos, this one with better news. Hans Bethe, head of the theoretical physics division, had spent Saturday analyzing the theory of the magnetic experiment. He concluded that the instrumental design was such that even a perfect implosion might produce oscilloscope records similar to those observed. So we were back at square one and I was forgiven at headquarters.

Despite the predictions of failure, on Saturday Bacher and his people had proceeded to insert the plutonium into the Gadget, an operation which also did not go quite smoothly. The plutonium assembly, previously carefully checked for size, now would not fit into the cavity at the center of the pit. Fortunately, they realized that this assembly, which was stored in an elaborately padded box, had become hot due to its radioactivity and therefore had expanded. Cooling it in open air did the trick and the delayed insertion was successful. Then Norris Bradbury and a couple of our GI.s replaced those explosives castings which had to be taken out in order to get into the pit The five-foot spherical Gadget was hoisted to the top of the hundred-foot tower, the kind that is used on oil wells. When placed, it was covered by a tin roof, shielding it from sun and lightning.

On Sunday, after Bethe's message eliminated Oppenheimer· s doubts about going ahead with the test, Hornig installed a fresh X unit on the Gadget and Henry Linschitz, another of my "youngsters," with the help of one of our G.I.s inserted the detonators into their sockets. Finally, Hornig connected the wires to the X unit. I just hung around on the top of that flimsy steel tower, not looking down because of vertigo but serving more or less as a witness that everything was done right. After climbing down the rungs, I had nothing more to do, so I took a jeep drove far into the desert, to soothe my nerves and to look for rare cacti, of which I found a few.

Sunday night, unexpectedly, I spent sitting part way up the bomb tower while Bainbridge and two others were on the ground just below me. The test scheduled for Sunday evening had to be delayed due to bad weather and General Groves insisted that there was danger of sabotage to the bomb, since the military guards had been withdrawn to assure their safety. So our group went to watch it, the commander of our Military Police clutching a submachine gun, Bainbridge on the phone to the control bunker, and I occasionally sweeping the countryside with a searchlight.

The decision to fire was conveyed to us shortly before 5:30 a.m. It was still dark. We started back, but first Bainbridge unlocked a box at the base of the tower which housed an open safety switch on the firing line from the control bunker to the X unit. All of us solemnly watched as Bainbridge closed the switch and locked the box. We got into the jeep, drove a mile, repeated the operation on the second safety switch, this one in a box in a trench, and so arrived at the control bunker 10,000 yards away. There Bainbridge opened still another locked box and closed the last safety switch. The Gadget was now ready to be remotely armed and fired.

The countdown began. Various measuring and photographic instruments were activated on schedule. A minute before time zero the automatic timer took over. According to contemporary accounts "a simple G.I." stood with his hand on the safety switch, ready to stop the sequence. It was really Hornig, but the khakis made us all look alike. The bunker was crowded, although

154

Oppenheimer made the visiting big shots stay back at the base camp where they were all lying in shallow trenches. I had no further duties, so before the count came to zero I went outside and to the top of the bunker, put on dark glasses and turned away from the tower so as not to be blinded. Although I was confident that implosion would work, I didn't think anything could happen to me because I was sure that the predictions of the theoretical physicists at Los Alamos greatly exaggerated the violence of the resulting nuclear reaction. I expected an explosion perhaps like that of the 100-ton charge of TNT that we had fired at the Trinity site a few weeks earlier to check out some of the site equipment. But I was as wrong about the implosion as the G division was on Saturday. I lost my bet in a large pool that was organized before Trinity. The nuclear reaction went off, the flash lit the countryside like a hundred suns, and the reflection from the far away mountains near blinded me for a few seconds. As I turned to the tower huge billowing clouds of dust spread from the base of the expanding fireball that rapidly became yellow, then red and finally became a mushroom cloud which ascended into the stratosphere. Meanwhile almost the whole sky lit with an intense violet glow. Quite incredible, that spectacle, so I forgot about the blast wave that hit and shook me quite a few seconds later. Now Oppenheimer and a few others were on the top of the bunker, some in silent awe, others in wild enthusiasm.

William L. Laurance, the official reporter of the Manhattan District Project, who watched the Trinity test from 20 miles away. wrote in the New York Times, September 26, 1945, of his experience: "It was as though the earth had opened and the skies had split. One felt as though he had been privileged to witness the Birth of the World-to be present at the moment of creation when the Lord said: 'Let there be light.'" To me he attributed a somber reaction: "I am sure that at the end of the world—in the last millisecond of the earth's existence—the last human will see what we saw." The big shots at the ranch were appropriately congratulatory later on, but that was the anticlimax. Before the day was over, I was back in Los Alamos to get the X division going on building the next Gadget. Almost a month later it exploded over Nagasaki.

George B. Kistiakowsky was professor of chemistry, emeritus, at Harvard University. He was Special Assistant for Science and Technology under President Eisenhower from July 1959 to January 1961, and a member of the President's Science Advisory Committee from 1957 to 1964.

Appendix 3
Nagasaki, the Second Bomb
By
Ellen Wilder Bradbury-Reid and Paula Schreiber
Dransfield

No other human activity is so continuously or
universally bound up with chance. And through the
element of chance, guesswork and luck come to play a
great part in war. (Von Clausewitz)

In 1945 the United States dropped two atomic bombs on
Japan. The first hit Hiroshima and the second Nagasaki.
The first bomb was a uranium bomb with a "gun" or impact
detonator; the second, a plutonium bomb, had a more
powerful and complex detonator. The dramatic story of the
second bomb, Fat Man, was lost between the shock of the
Hiroshima bomb and the surrender of Japan.

This second bomb came into being through two
miscalculations. The first was that the uranium plant in Oak
Ridge, Tennessee would not be able to produce enough of
the uranium isotope U235 to make more than one bomb
within the militarily imposed deadline. The second
occurred when the plutonium isotope Pu239 from Hanford,
Washington arrived at Los Alamos inexorably combined
with Pu240, polluting the isotope and producing detonation
instability that prevented using the simple gun "impact"
method proposed for both the uranium and plutonium
bombs.

157

The scientists at Los Alamos were suddenly faced with a complicated technical problem, a huge setback for a project that was on a fast track. They had to figure out how to make a bomb using the massively expensive plutonium. One physicist, Seth Neddermeyer, had taken a highly unorthodox approach to creating an implosion bomb by developing a method to "squeeze" the plutonium into a smaller and denser critical mass. The theory was that if the metal were "squeezed" hard enough, the plutonium would first implode and then explode. Other physicists had ridiculed his research until it became their salvation.

Suddenly all effort was focused to make Neddermeyer's idea work, although the concept was so convoluted and complex that the military took the time to test this new "gadget" on July 16, 1945, at Trinity Site on White Sands Missile Range in southern New Mexico. Much to everyone's relief, the test proved the implosion gadget worked. The gadget was an oversized, ungainly, mainly round, impossible to aim creature soon dubbed the "Fat Man." It's bloated 59-inch circumference was limited only by the fact that it somehow had to be delivered and the largest bomb bay available was the 62-inch width of the B-29 super fortress. Fat Man would eventually be launched with one and a half inches of clearance.

The problem of dropping one huge bomb with little information about what would happen when it exploded was handed to the 509th Composite Group led by Colonel Paul Tibbets. Tibbets worked with navy Commander Frederick Ashworth who shuttled back and forth between Wendover Army Air Force Base and Los Alamos to help Tibbets figure out how to drop the giant ball and then get out of the way. Tibbets and Ashworth had been at Trinity and knew the power of this new weapon but no one else in the 509th knew what the bomb was. Tibbets practiced by dropping dummy bombs referred to as "pumpkins" that instead of dropping straight like a cylindrical bomb rolled in the air. Ashworth and Tibbets finally solved the rolling problem by welding an open box on one end of the ball to funnel the air to stabilize the bomb's descent.

The success of the Trinity Site explosion finalized the political decision to use the atomic bombs on Japan. Duplicates of the Fat Man casings had been optimistically shipped to Tinian Island in the Mariannas weeks before the Trinity test. The plutonium core for Fat Man was to be sent by airplane. In all, one ship, five C-54s, and three B-29s were dispatched to carry various parts of the two bombs.

The ship was the *Indianapolis*, an older vessel lacking submarine detection instruments, carried the heavy bomb casings. On July 29, after delivering the cargo and departing Tinian the *Indianapolis* was hit by a Japanese torpedo and sunk. Some men were drowned immediately, and of the almost 850 who got off the ship only 318 men survived.

Back in Los Alamos, the Trinity bomb assembly crew drew straws to see who would have the job of escorting the plutonium core to Tinian. Raemer Schreiber (Schreib), a junior member of the nuclear assembly crew, drew the short straw. On July 25, he flew out of Albuquerque on a C-54 cargo plane to hand-carry the core (nicknamed "Rufus") to Tinian. Part way through the flight, Schreib had worked his way up to the cockpit to get a better picture of the turbulence they were experiencing, leaving "Rufus," he thought, securely attached to a metal brace. It wasn't long before one of the crew members notified him that the mechanism was rolling around in the back of the plane. After that, Rufus and Schreib were inseparable. While the crew didn't know exactly what they were carrying, they knew it had to be dangerous because the big plane was empty except for the scientist, a squad of MPs, a security escort, and this thing that looked like a car battery shoved into a wire milk bottle basket. The empty cargo plane caused considerable consternation at Hickham Field in Hawaii when the plane was declared off limits to supply clerks desperate to send medical supplies to the islands.

Schreib and the plutonium core arrived on Tinian on July 28 Tinian time. He was one of a team of about 50 scientists sent to "destination" whose jobs were to make sure the bombs worked. While no one knew when the bombs would be dropped and some hoped that no bombs would be used, the teams, including the nuclear assembly team headed by Captain William S. "Deke" Parsons and his second, Commander Frederick Ashworth, started through the long procedures to ensure both bombs would be ready.

The waiting was frustrating. There was only so much that could be done for bomb pre-assembly, the monsoon season dumped inches of rain every day, B-29s were taking off and landing constantly, and the only entertainment was an outdoor theater. Schreib and the team members watched movies like *This is the Army* (Irving Berlin and Peggy Lee) and *Hotel Berlin* through curtains of rain protected by helmet liners and raincoats, sitting on soggy canvas stools. Schreib said they were also warned casually that they should not stare if they saw a Jap soldier in the brush because there were still some on the island and he might shoot if he thought he was seen. Forced to wear army uniforms, physicists who had never learned to salute worried that the Japanese would see their inexperience and know they weren't military, so practice time for saluting became part of the daily routine.

One cloudy day the scientists watched in awe as hundreds of ships hove to in the lee of the Marianas to avoid a storm. Schreiber said, "You could walk from deck to deck all the way to the horizon without getting your feet wet." They were told it was the allied invasion force. If Washington decided not to use the bomb, or if the bomb failed, it would be up to the men on those hundreds of ships to end the war.

But the use of the bomb had to wait on the weather. B-29s flew in all kinds of weather, but a new wrinkle had been added to this particular mission.

On the evening of July 23 . . . [Oppenheimer] met with General Farrell and his aide, Lt. Col. John F. Moynahan, two senior officers designated to supervise the bombing run over Hiroshima from the island of Tinian. It was a clear, cool, starry night. Pacing nervously in his office, chain-smoking, Oppenheimer wanted to make sure that they understood his precise instructions for delivering the weapon on target. Lieutenant Colonel Moynahan, a former newspaperman, published a vivid account of the evening in a 1946 pamphlet: " 'Don't let them bomb through clouds or through an overcast,' [Oppenheimer said.] He was emphatic,

161

tense, his nerves talking. 'Got to see the target. No radar bombing; it must be dropped visually.' Long strides, feet turned out, another cigarette. 'Of course, it doesn't matter if they check the drop with radar, but it must be a visual drop.' More strides. 'If they drop it at night there should be a moon; that would be best. Of course, they must not drop it in rain or fog . . . Don't let them detonate it too high. The figure fixed on is right. Don't let it go up [higher] or the target won't get as much damage . . .' "

General Groves, the military director of the Manhattan Project, decided to use Little Boy, the gun detonator uranium bomb, first because he had more confidence in that weapon. If only one bomb was to be dropped there could be no error. Even though Fat Man had been tested, he was concerned that the enormous technical problems of the plutonium bomb made it more subject to possible failure.

By August 4 the go-ahead for the Little Boy had everyone scrambling to ensure a smooth operation. While Schreib's team had no direct responsibility for the Little Boy, there was much tension, especially when there was a last-minute change in procedure to load the propellant that assembled the bomb after the plane was airborne. Captain Parsons took on the assignment and crawled into the *Enola Gay's* bomb bay after takeoff.

So on August 6, the *Enola Gay* took off with Paul Tibbets as pilot, made the appointed rendezvous at Iwo Jima with the support planes, made a perfect flight to Japan, saw Hiroshima, dropped the bomb, and returned to

Tinian where the scientists and technicians were waiting. Colonel Tibbets was awarded the Distinguished Service Cross almost as soon as he landed. Later that afternoon Tibbets addressed the assembled 509th personnel and broke the news that the first nuclear bomb had been delivered. This was the first time that many of them knew what their whole mission was about.

The United States was anxious to use the second bomb, both to convince the Japanese to surrender and to justify the investment of $2 billion for the project. Politically, the implosion bomb needed to be used because if Japan surrendered, it might be hard to convince Congress that the expenditures had been necessary. Several U.S. officials felt it would take two bombs to convince the Japanese military that the Hiroshima bomb was not a one-time freak event.

With the decision to drop the second bomb, the monsoon weather became a problem since reliable weather reports depended on data from the Soviet Union, which had suddenly become a reluctant partner in the war. Japanese weather often originates over Siberia and while the Soviet Union was technically an ally, they did not relay any weather reports to the anxious group at Tinian. The Soviets were in the process of invading Manchuria and wanted to prolong the war long enough to move their army. With no weather information coming from the Soviets, the U.S. was left to its own devices. On Tinian the plutonium core and the large pumpkin casing waited for the clouds over Japan to lift. Only one day of good weather was forecast: August 9. The next five days were to be cloudy.

On August 6, the assembly crew was ordered to proceed with the preparation of Fat Man. "We were somewhat surprised that the order to drop the second bomb was given only three days later," Schreiber said. "We had all hoped Japan would give some indication of surrender and call it quits." They weren't prepared for the impossibly short time to finish the assembly and warned Captain Parsons that they would have to eliminate several checkout procedures. The crew, including Schreib, started the slow and somewhat nerve-wracking process of lowering the plutonium plug that he had babysat across the ocean into the bomb assembly. The plug had to be lowered microns at a time while the neutron level was monitored. The nuclear assembly was designed to be at 95 percent of critical when completely inserted. Once that was completed, neutron measurements had to continue to ensure that the background level was within tolerance. The measurements continued until the early hours before takeoff on August 9.

According to Schreib:

> It was decided that there should be some sort of disaster plan in case of a crash at takeoff. It was not possible to "safe" the Fat Man, so a crash would almost certainly cause the HE (High Explosives) to explode and scatter plutonium even if there were no nuclear explosion. Our little group had essentially all the radiation detectors and most of the know-how so it became our responsibility to develop an emergency plan . . . In case of a crash, we were to rush out with our monitoring instruments and establish safe limits for entry. We were now a part of the strike operation and were therefore participants in the pre-strike briefing.

This made the night of August 8 a very short night.

Bernard J. O'Keefe remembered "Living on that island, with planes going out every night and people dying not only in B-29s shot down, but in naval engagements all over the Pacific, we knew the importance of (even) one day; the Indianapolis sinking also had a strong effect on us." He went on to tell his story of the last check out he did on Fat Man.

> When I returned at midnight, the others in my group left to get some sleep. I was alone in the assembly room with a single Army technician to make the final connection. . . I did my final checkout and reached for the cable to plug it into the firing nit. It wouldn't fit. I must be doing something wrong, I thought. Go slowly; you're tired and must not be thinking straight.
>
> I looked again. To my horror, there was a female plug on the firing set and a female plug on the cable. I walked around the weapon and looked at the radars and the other end of the cable. Two male plugs . . . I checked and double-checked. I had the technician check; he verified my findings. I felt a chill and started to sweat in the air-conditioned room. What had happened was obvious. In the rush to take advantage of good weather, someone had gotten careless and put the cable in backward.

O'Keefe decided to improvise by unsoldering the connectors from the two ends of the cable, reversing them and re-soldering them. But first, he had to find an electrical outlet; there was one in the next room. He finally found two long extension cords that would reach into the assembly room if he braced the door open. "I resoldered the plugs onto the other ends of the cable, keeping as much distance between the soldering iron and the detonators as I could." If he had waited and followed safety procedures the flight would have had to be cancelled.

B-29s were the largest planes anywhere, but the distance from Tinian to the Japanese mainland, 1,272 miles one way, was at the farthest limit of the plane's capabilities. Fat Man was very heavy, 10,000 pounds, 1,100 pounds more than Little Boy, the bomb dropped on Hiroshima. These big planes also had a habit of catching on fire on takeoff from the sputtering fuel and sparks from the engines; many B-29 planes crashed on takeoff. The B-29s were notorious for individual idiosyncrasies that each crew learned to work with and around, making each B-29 the special provenance of its assigned crew.

Major Charles Sweeney had been designated to fly the second bomb run, but because of the short timeline between the first and second bomb, Sweeney's plane, *The Great Artiste*, was still configured as an instrument plane. Tibbets decided to switch crews, putting Sweeney in Bock's plane, and Captain Frederick C. Bock in *The Great Artiste*.

Commander Ashworth, the man assigned as the "weaponeer" for the second bomb run, was concerned when he learned that Colonel Tibbits had assigned Major Charles Sweeney to fly Captain Bock's plane.

Sweeney's crew was not completely familiar with the idiosyncrasies of the *Bockscar*. For example, Sweeney's flight engineer could not transfer the gasoline that was in the bomb bay into the main system. [However,] Tibbets was the final authority on the mission and he told Sweeney that if the operation ran according to the schedule, there should be no problem.

With the jammed fuel line, the weather, and the heavy load, Sweeney and Tibbets decided to change the flight plan by adding a refueling stop at Yontan Airfield, Okinawa. Afraid of missing the window of good weather, *Bockscar* took off at 0347 on August 9.

Bockscar's crew was dressed in regulation gray flight suits with no identifying insignia. Flight Engineer Ray Gallagher wrote in his diary: "As we walked past the last bed, the barracks bag was laying [sic] there. When we passed the bag and dropped our wallets inside, truthfully, I never thought I'd pick it up again."

Raemer Schreiber stood at the end of the runway as the plane lumbered the full length of the strip dodging lightning-laden clouds. "I don't know what I could have done if there was a problem," he remembered.

There were a total of five B-29s on the second atomic mission. Two aircraft launched one hour before the bomb-carrying plane, one to go to the area of the primary target, Kokura, and one to the secondary target, Nagasaki, to observe and report the weather to the plane carrying the bomb. There were three B-29s in the "Attack Element": the *Great Artiste* commanded by Bock to carry Los Alamos bomb yield instruments and the Los Alamos scientists who would monitor them, the *Big Stink* piloted by Major James I. Hopkins with the British observers and the cameras, and *Bockscar*, carrying the bomb.

In the first few hours of the flight some of the men slept. With Sweeney as commander, pilot 1st Lt Charles D. Albury and co-pilot 2nd Lt Fred J. Olivi took turns flying the long distance to the Japanese mainland. Because of a typhoon over Iwo Jima, the rendezvous point for the three planes had been changed to the small island of Yakashima. There was bad weather all night.

At 07:00 a red light on the instrument panel monitoring the bomb called the Black Box began to flash wildly. This indicated that the bomb was fully armed and could detonate at any moment. For ten frantic minutes Lt. Philip M. Barnes and Ashworth studied the bomb blueprints and dug into the wiring diagram to figure out what was going on and reverse it. Finally Barnes discovered two switches had been improperly set. He reset the switches and the red light settled into a slow blinking. Barnes spent the rest of the flight watching the light to make sure it didn't start to blink rapidly again.

Because the U.S. meteorologists had been unable to make accurate forecasts of the weather, the expected poor weather was already in place when the three planes assigned to the flight tried to rendezvous over the southeast coast of Kyushu. Radio silence was absolute, so they had no way to contact each other. At 09:00 both *Bockscar* and the *Great Artiste* arrived at the rendezvous point. Sweeney recorded: "We had navigated through bad, black weather all night long. There was the most terrible storm. We went to 17,000 feet because we wanted to get the smoothest air we could get. After five hours we went up to 30,000 feet to rendezvous . . ."

Ashworth, who had control of the bombing mission as weaponeer, thought that Hopkins, flying the instrument plane, had been delayed by the bad weather. However, Hopkins was there, over the right island but at the wrong altitude, 9,000 feet above them. "Little wonder that he did not see us," said Ashworth.

Hopkins flew around for a few minutes looking for *Bockscar* and then, panicking, did the unthinkable. He breached the mandatory radio silence with the awful question: "Had 77 (that is Sweeney's plane, *Bockscar*, with the bomb) aborted?" The message was slightly garbled; at Tinian what they as heard was "77 aborted." Had *Bockscar* crashed or been shot down, did it jettison the bomb, and where was the crew? As a result, it was more than two hours before they learned that the mission had actually succeeded, and as a further result the rescue ships and planes for that mission were canceled.

When Hopkins' message was received at Tinian, General Farrell ran outside his tent and "lost his cookies."

Meanwhile in the air over Yakashima there was a debate in the cockpit. Should they continue to wait for the other plane and fly a perfect mission? It is not clear why Sweeney did not tell Ashworth that the plane that did arrive at Yakashima was the instrument plane, the *Great Artiste*, the plane they needed to make the calculations on the yield of the bomb. From where Ashworth was sitting, back from the cockpit next to the bomb, he could not actually see the other plane. Ashworth knew the instrument plane was the important plane and so assumed that Sweeney was waiting for it; had he known that the plane with them was the instrument plane, he would have ordered them on immediately.

In Ashworth's words,

> We waited and waited for the last plane . . . We continued to fly around for 45 minutes. Sweeney had in mind that we were supposed to have three airplanes going to the target. I think he wanted a perfect operation. The net result was we wasted 45 minutes of precious gasoline.

With the plane redirected, Ashworth continues:

> We approached (the first target) Kokura. We could not see the target. We had specific orders that we had to drop the bomb visually. . . We tried three runs to drop the bomb visually without a success and that took 55 minutes. We decided to try the second target, Nagasaki.

Ashworth knew they had to change the plan immediately if they were going to drop the bomb. If they didn't drop the bomb they would have to ditch at sea and hope to be picked up. This was not a very good prospect since they were now directly over the Japanese mainland. And they were carrying the most expensive and devastating weapon ever devised; their job was to deliver it. Ashworth moved forward in the plane to talk to Sweeney in the cockpit. They were dangerously low on fuel. Sweeney was reluctant to change the original plan.

Finally, Ashworth prevailed and they headed for their second target, Nagasaki. Because of the low fuel, they sent a coded message to alert the air-sea rescue team that they might have to ditch. (They could not know, of course, that the rescue had been canceled by Hopkins' call back to Tinian.) To save fuel they flew directly over the island of Kyushu, a more dangerous route than the originally prescribed over-water route, because they were exposed to anti-aircraft fire.

Reflecting the mounting tension in the plane, Lt. Olivi wrote:

> Reducing power to save gas—wonder if the Pacific will be cold? Our chances for ditching are good. Bomb must be dropped for more reasons than one. Hope it goes off. It'll be a hell of a lot of sweating for nothing if it don't. 11:40 Boys are getting jittery. Can't blame them.

As they approached Nagasaki at 11:50 it appeared at first that the city was covered in clouds. Ashworth knew that they'd been ordered to make a visual drop to ensure they hit the correct target, but contrary to these orders Ashworth decided that radar was their only chance to complete the mission. He told the bombardier to follow the radar approach as closely as possible and be prepared to switch over for a visual run if conditions changed. If they did not, Ashworth said to release the bomb by radar: he would take responsibility. Ashworth continues:

We had only one chance. I feel that it was my responsibility to try a radar approach. We did not have enough gasoline to get (back) to Tinian. . . We could not even make it to Okinawa. The alternative was to drop the bomb in the water or to ditch the plane with the bomb.

So they went with a radar approach over Nagasaki. Ashworth was prepared to take the hit for dropping the bomb by instrument, but he said:

It turned out the 20 seconds before the bombardier, (Captain Kermit) Breen, dropped the bomb he could see the target through an opening of clouds. . . He began a count down and then said "Bombs Away." The bomb went off right over the Mitsubishi Arms and Steel Works.

At 11:58, Fat Man exploded with a force estimated at 22 kilotons. The hills around Nagasaki produced five shock waves; *Bockscar* banked and turned; looking back, the crew could see the mushroom cloud rising.

The pilots had been given welder's glasses to protect their eyes from the bomb's light, but they could not see the instrument panel with the glasses so did not wear them. Lt. Olivi said:

It was a bright bluish color. It took about 45 or 50 seconds to get up to our altitude and then continued on up. We could see the bottom of the mushroom stem. It was a boiling cauldron. Salmon pink was the predominant color . . . we couldn't see anything down there because it was smoke and fire all over the area where the city was. Everybody was concentrating down there and I remember the mushroom cloud was on our left. Somebody . . . hollered in the back "the mushroom cloud is coming toward us." This is when Sweeney took the aircraft and dove it down to the right, full throttle, and I remember looking at the damn thing on our left and I couldn't tell for a while whether it was gaining on us or we were gaining on it.

Strangely enough, Hopkins, who had missed the rendezvous at Yakashima, appeared over Nagasaki in time to see the mushroom cloud. He had flown on after his message back to Tinian, and saw that the mission had not aborted but was a success. He saw the bomb go off over Nagasaki from a distance, flew there to observe the location of the burst, estimated the damage, and then proceeded to Okinawa. His plane and the *Great Artiste* had access to the extra fuel stored in their wings and were not in the extreme distress that *Bockscar* was.

After the bomb was dropped the *Bockscar*'s fuel gauge showed 300 gallons. With the weight of the bomb gone it might be possible to reach Okinawa 150 miles away, but the plane was in trouble. Onboard they knew they might not make it, but they continued to maintain radio silence except for a coded "MAYDAY" as they left the coast of Japan. The crew put on their life jackets and prepared to ditch. They glided down to 5,000 feet to save what fuel they had.

The crew flew in silence, each man worrying about Japanese aircraft, each wondering if they were going to make it. Finally they saw the island of Okinawa ahead. Recently under American control and used as an airbase very close to the Japanese mainland, Okinawa was a very active airbase. They could see it and were almost there with all fuel tanks reading empty.

Sweeney knew he had only one shot at this landing. Adjusting the plane as they approached, Sweeney tried to raise the tower. Lt. Olivi remembers:

> It was a real busy field. We made our radio calls and got no answer. We called it four times in hopes of getting our landing instructions and letting them know our situation. They didn't come back to us and that's when Sweeney decided to declare a Mayday. He told me, "Fire all the flares. We're going in." I was in the navigator/radio compartment. I took out the flare gun, stuck it out the porthole at the top of the fuselage and fired the flares we had, one after another. There were about eight or ten of them. Each color indicated a specific condition onboard the aircraft.
>
> The field started to clear in a big hurry. Sweeney broke into the traffic pattern and cut out three or four aircraft that were already on approach so he could make the landing.

Lt. Albury, the second pilot on the mission, takes up the narrative:

> [The] #2 engine stopped just before touchdown. We immediately put the engines in reverse and slammed on the brakes. The aircraft veered to the left . . . Sweeney compensated by pulling back on #1 engine in reverse and increased the brakes on the right side and [by] releasing some of the pressure on the left brakes. I know because I was on the brakes with him.

And then Olivi:

> We hit the runway at about 140 or 150 mph, much too fast to hit the ground safely. We started to veer off to the left and if it weren't for the reversible props we would have taken out a slew of aircraft. They were parked away from the active runway, but they were still there. If we would have continued out of control we would have smacked into them. Sweeney straightened it out and continued down the runway.

They came to a roaring but safe stop about fifty feet from the end of the runway. As they taxied to the operations line the two outboard engines stopped from fuel starvation.

When they measured the remaining fuel on *Bockscar* there were either 7 or 35 gallons left. On a B-29, that's called empty.

Appendix 4

Vital Connections

By Richard Rhodes

When Robert Oppenheimer recruited scientists for the new secret Laboratory under construction on the grounds of the former Los Alamos Ranch School, he was restricted by the requirements of national security form telling them what their work would be. So he found an equivalent that appealed to their patriotism and altruism. He walked them out across their campuses at Harvard and Wisconsin and Berkeley and Columbia and whispered to them that the work he was inviting them to join "would probably end this war and might end all war."

I'm sure you're familiar with the seemingly endless debate about the bombing of Hiroshima and Nagasaki. Was it to end the war? Was it to try out a new weapon? Was it to scare the Russians? Did it end the war? I usually take the position that most of the various arguments that historians have raised are all correct. It was to end the war. It was to try out a new weapon. It was to scare the Russians. It did end the war, if the Emperor of Japan is to be believed; in his Imperial rescript asking his people to lay down their arms he specifically cited what he called "a new and most terrible weapon of war" as the reason he and they should accept the unthinkable.

What was the social reality in the summer of 1945? We had been at war since the end of 1941, four long years, years of terrible loss of life, more lives lost worldwide than in any previous war in history, loss of life comparable to the devastation of some unsurpassed great plague end every one of those lives a loss of love, of relation, of human potential, of another part of human innocence as well. The Russians with our help and British help had finally beaten the Nazis.

We had destroyed the Japanese Navy and Air Force and blockaded the Japanese home islands; they had a year's supply of ammunition on hand but very little food. We considered them defeated, but they steadfastly refused to surrender on our terms and seemed to be prepared to fight for their homeland down to the last man, woman and child – until they said, until we eat stones.

Was Oppenheimer also right about the work at Los Alamos ending all war? On first inspection he would seem to have been wrong. Obviously there have been wars since 1945. But look more closely, and form a longer perspective, and I think the question might have a different answer.

Imagine a graph. The vertical scale is man-made deaths-deaths from war and war's attendant privation – in millions. The horizontal scale is years, starting in 1900. After 1945 we see nothing like the steep spikes of the two world wars. Just as public health brought most of the epidemic diseases under increasing social control, in the West during the first half of the 20th century, so does it appear that something brought man-made death under increasing social control in the second half of the 20th century.

In the long run, Robert Oppenheimer may turn out to have been right with both of his predictions.

Richard Rhodes Copyright 2001

Pulitzer prize-winning author. The making of the Atomic Bomb, Dark Sun, and 18 other books.

Appendix 5

SEDs at Los Alamos: A Personal Memoir

Benjamin Bederson

Excerpts from an article originally published in Physics in Perspective, 2001

Benjamin Bederson was a Professor of Physics Emeritus at New York University and Editor-in-Chief Emeritus, American Physical Society.

I have written this personal memoir approximately 55 years after the events I describe. It is based almost exclusively on memory, since apart from the diary I kept while on Tinian, I have few documents concerning it. It covers my service in the U.S. Army's Special Engineering Detachment (SED) in Oak Ridge and Los Alamos in 1944–45, on Tinian Island, the launching pad for the bombing raids on Japan, in the summer and fall of 1945, and my return to Los Alamos until my discharge in January 1946.

The role played by the common U.S. soldier in the development of atomic weapons during World War II is not generally appreciated. Early in the history of the Manhattan Project, the U.S. Army decided to tap the vast pool of GIs possessing scientific and technical backgrounds who were serving in it, mostly as draftees. These soldiers were assigned to an entity called the Special Engineering Detachment, and hence were known as ''SEDs.'' Their ranks also included skilled mechanics, machinists, and electronic technicians. At its peak in 1945 about 1800 SEDs were working, mainly at the principal Manhattan

Project sites at Los Alamos and Oak Ridge. The main role of the SEDs was to act as assistants – something like graduate students – to the senior scientists who by then were arriving at Los Alamos and Oak Ridge in large numbers. They were assigned to the many individual research projects that would eventually culminate in the successful design and construction of the two atomic bombs, the "Little Boy" and the "Fat Man," as well as to the various technical shops. Often little distinction was made between people in and out of uniform, although the former were subject to army regulations and discipline, as well as to army salaries rather than civilian ones. As work progressed, many of these soldiers assumed positions of considerable importance while still being subject to normal army routines, tempered somewhat by the rather loose discipline that prevailed, particularly toward the end of the war.

Army Life at Los Alamos

All SEDs were assigned to a special barracks; other soldiers such as MPs and guards were quartered elsewhere. (When I arrived there was only one SED barracks, although a second was soon built.) There was an interesting dichotomy in our daily lives. While working in the Tech Area or elsewhere we were treated like the civilian workers, with privileges compatible to our jobs and responsibilities. However, at other times we were simply soldiers like all other soldiers, with a lieutenant in charge of the SEDs and a major in charge of all soldiers. Our officer in charge did not have access to bomb information, and this caused significant tension, since his authority was strictly limited. For example, if a soldier had to work at night, or was traveling, he could easily get out of normal routine. This did not prevent the lieutenant from imposing Army discipline to the extent he could. At first we had to submit to early morning drill and calisthenics, before going to work. This was exceedingly unpopular among the SEDs, and was eventually done away with. We had to abide by normal barracks' discipline, which mainly meant Saturday morning inspections. Depending on who happened to be the commanding officer, these were either cursory or strict. We of course took these impositions as lightly as possible. We had to keep our footlockers in prime shape, clothing and toilet articles clean and neat, and shoes highly shined. At one particular inspection, to show our contempt for this kind of treatment, my bunkmate and I polished the soles of our shoes and exhibited them bottom side up. Unfortunately, the CO took no notice. Cigarettes were also required to be neatly stacked. On another occasion I put a box in my footlocker labeled ''opium for smoking,'' but again this elicited no reaction.

I have to admit that the Army and I were never really meant for each other. Looking back, I am quite aware that my own free-wheeling bringing up in the Bronx and Brighton Beach (Brooklyn) was poor preparation for Army life. I now believe that painful as it was at the time the discipline and routines of this life were crucial in helping me later to complete graduate school and develop a career in physics. Many aspects of Army discipline at Los Alamos did not sit well with me, and, need I add, visa versa. I was not a spit-and-polish soldier, and I was continually getting into hot water with my commanding officer about my dress and appearance. Many other SEDs had similar problems. One of my close friends and barracks neighbor was Dick Davisson, son of the famous physicist C.J. Davisson of Davisson and Germer fame. Dick was as bad as I was. He devised a method that would not require him to ever make his bed. He simply made it once, and then slept on top of it, with a thin blanket to cover him. He bragged that that was the only time he made his bed during his entire residence at Los Alamos.

I was always homesick for New York, and on one occasion was so homesick that I tied a bagel to the overhead light string next to my bunk. (The bagel was given to me by Peter Lax, later to become a most distinguished mathematician, who had received it in a package from home.) Val Fitch, a fellow SED, wrote about this incident in his own memoir of SED days called "A view from the bottom," published in the Bulletin of the Atomic Scientists in 1975. My bunkmate (he had the upper one) was William Spindel, a chemist with a degree from Brooklyn College, later to become an officer of the National Academy of Sciences National Research Council, who worked on gaseous diffusion, that is, isotope separation. He originally had introduced himself to me because he had heard of my presence at Los Alamos from a mutual New York friend. At first the double-decker next to ours was occupied by a New York machinist, David Greenglass, along with a New York friend of his, also a machinist, whose name I do not recall. It did not take long for them to reveal their political sympathies, which were nothing but those of communists, plain and simple. Bill and I, however, had long shed our earlier pro-Soviet sympathies, and political arguments among the four of us gradually grew more intemperate. Eventually they became so unpleasant that Bill and I asked for and received permission to transfer to the second, newly constructed barracks. At first security was so tight that we were not permitted to leave the post. Some time in late 1945 we were allowed to visit Santa Fe. Eventually we even were permitted to go to Albuquerque, where wives of GIs also were permitted to live. A number of my New York friends were married and soon a virtual colony of SED wives was established there. Among them were the wives of Richard Bellman and David Greenglass. Bellman was a mathematician of considerable talent and later fame. On weekends I would often take a bus from Santa Fe to Albuquerque. Occasionally I would ride with Richard Feynman, who was already by this time an acknowledged genius, and a luminous star of the theoretical division (he was a very young civilian--not an SED). He would travel to Albuquerque every weekend to visit his wife, extremely ill, dying of tuberculosis. He had no compunctions about complaining about Los Alamos security and bureaucracy, which he expressed in a loud voice, unafraid. I was not so bold, being in uniform, and cringed from time to time in hearing him sound off. Of course he never got into any trouble about this.

Barracks' life was not unlike the experiences of millions of other GIs during the war. As already noted, we had neither latrine duty nor KP – these were performed by hired local women, Mexican and Indian. But living in one large room with 49 other soldiers was hardly a pleasant experience. The latrines were public, as were the showers. Heat was supplied by two or three coal stoves per barracks, and these had to be stoked by volunteers, especially in the early morning when it tended to be very cold. I had to perform my share of this onerous chore. Of course none of us, including me, really resented our lot. We were all too well aware that there were soldiers fighting and dying while we had to suffer relatively unimportant inconveniences, while performing exciting and important work. Thus, our gripes were not taken very seriously, either by the Army or by ourselves. Probably the most serious complaint the SEDs had concerned relative rather than absolute treatment. Young civilians and SEDs (and even some Navy Ensigns) often worked side by side with comparable responsibilities, sometimes with SEDs ranking higher than civilians. But the civilians not only did not have to put up with Army discipline, they also were far better paid. This did not make very good sense to the GIs whose monthly checks often did not reach higher than two digits. In late spring of 1945, I received a letter from my father framed in black ink. He informed me that my close friend Irving Yusin, who had shared living quarters with me in Philadelphia for six months before I was drafted in 1942, had been killed in the Battle of the Bulge.

This essentially trivialized my so-called hardships, putting them into the proper perspective of the year 1944. SEDs would sometimes be called upon to perform other duties, notably helping to put out forest fires. The dry New Mexico climate resulted in frequent small fires in the pine forests surrounding Los Alamos. From time to time we would be "recruited" to go on forest fire duty. I didn't object to this very much, except on occasion when after a hard day (and night) stint doing timing tests we would be awakened to help put one out. I developed a strategy to avoid such duty after particularly long hours – I would hike from Two Mile Mesa to the back entrance to Los Alamos, slip through a rickety barbed-wire barrier, and seek out an ancient Indian cave in what is now the Bandolier National Monument. There I would luxuriate in a good night's sleep under a ceiling covered with the smoke of ancient cooking fires, with walls sometimes marked with equally ancient glyphs. And speaking of fires, there was a very serious fire in the Los Alamos machine shop, likely around April 1945. That time I grabbed a hose and entered the shop, becoming a bona fide fireman, braving the smoke and fire to help preserve the much-needed shop.

Furloughs, when they were given at all, were given grudgingly – not surprising in view of the Army's nervousness about security. I believe that in all I had maybe three furloughs, taking that interminable train ride from Lamy to New York. Of course I was not able to talk about my work to anyone, although surprisingly one or two of my friends made some pretty accurate guesses about what I was doing. In one case a friend told me of an experiment at the University of Chicago, even naming the football stadium as the location, where some hush-hush experiments concerning atomic bombs were taking place. This was long

187

before I knew anything about Enrico Fermi's reactor experiments. I have a letter from another artist friend who actually drew a picture of an atomic explosion for me, kidding me about what I was doing. Mail was censored both coming and going, although only the mail sent to me bore a censorship seal. Outgoing mail had to be unsealed, and passed by the censor. I had one censor assigned to me throughout my stay at Los Alamos, and after a while we developed a kind of friendship. To this day I have no idea who he (or she) was, though of course he (or she) knew all about me. In all of the time I was at Los Alamos I met its two principal leaders exactly once each. Shortly before Christmas 1944, I, along with a handful of other SEDs, were invited to meet with General Leslie R. Groves. Expecting something a bit more worldshaking at this momentous event (for a corporal), General Groves revealed his purpose in arranging the meeting. It was, he said, to urge us to write home to our parents at Christmas time. You have no idea, he said, how much this would mean to them. At the meeting he also asked whether we had any complaints or suggestions on how life could be made better for us. Only one SED spoke up – he was very unhappy that the Army did not supply us with adequate baseball equipment. We needed more balls, gloves, and bats. General Groves promised to look into it, and we adjourned.

The Army had established a point system based upon length of service, duty in combat areas, and other factors, for determining the order of priority in getting out. My designated time of discharge was late January 1946. Thus, I had a lot of time to kill (apart from my reactor-inspection duties, which were hardly onerous). I spent much of this time listening to music, traveling to Santa Fe and Albuquerque, and mainly playing Chinese Checkers with Richard Bellman. Living up to his brilliant reputation, he was a formidable adversary, although I did manage to beat him about a third of the time. We also had an ongoing game of hearts – a cutthroat game in the best of circumstances, with Bellman, Greenspan, myself, and Murray Peshkin as regular participants. (Peshkin is now a highly regarded Argonne physicist.) Greenspan reminds me that on one occasion after a particularly offensive play Peshkin chased him around the Tech Area late at night with a jagged tin can, but I can't personally vouch for this. More importantly, the administration had decided that it would be a good idea to have some of the many luminaries on the site offer "courses" – actually, lecture series, on topics in pure physics. I happily sat in on many of these, including ones by Edward Teller, Philip Morrison, Robert Serber (of "Serber Says" fame), and also some guest lectures by Hans Bethe, among others. Needless to say, these were wonderful preparation for my future graduate school studies. A final temptation was put in my path. Just before my discharge I was approached by one of my former group leaders who invited me to participate in the planned nuclear tests to take place in the South Pacific in 1946 and later. I was offered what to me seemed like an amazingly high salary – $6000 for six months. This was over sixty times what I was then earning as a soldier. Pleased with the flattery, I had no trouble turning it down, and instead proceeded with my plan to finish college at CCNY, and then go on to graduate school. Eventually my number came

189

up, I traveled to Fort Bliss, Texas, aptly named, and received my discharge.

It is virtually obligatory for any atom bomb memoir to include a discussion on the merits of President Harry S. Truman's decision to drop the bomb. I can take care of this obligation here by simply describing what I have told students at New York University whenever they would confront me with this question. I would point out that had the bombs not been used many of the men and women in the class would not be there, since one of their parents or grandparents would not have survived the inevitable invasion of Japan. This was, and is, a very compelling argument.

Strong Opinions

Rudolf Peierls painted a vivid picture of J. Robert Oppenheimer's likes and dislikes: He had strong views on questions of style in food and drink. Martinis had to be strong. Coffee had to be black. When coffee was served in their house, there was never any cream or sugar on the table. They would be provided on request, but the hosts started from the assumption that the guests would want to have their coffee the proper way. Steak had to be rare (underdone), and this brings a story to mind. Oppenheimer took the members of a committee to a steak house after a meeting. Everybody ordered steak, and the waiter took orders on how it should be cooked. Oppenheimer said "rare", and this was echoed by everybody in turn, until the waiter came to Robert's neighbor on the other side, who said "well done". Robert looked at him and said, "Why don't you have fish?"

Rudolf Peierls, Bird of Passage: Recollections of a Physicist (Princeton: Princeton University Press, 1985), pp. 189–190.

Appendix 6

On My Own
Dimas Chávez

The following is an excerpt from a book called On My Own. This interesting book is a memoir written by Dimas Chávez and published in 2014 on Amazon Press.

Dimas Chávez was born May 27, 1937, in a small town in central New Mexico called Torreon. His father was a small rancher, raising cattle and sheep. When World War II began with the attack of Pearl Harbor, it disrupted the community because most of the young men left to join the war effort. Dimas' father did not get drafted as the government viewed his job as a farmer/rancher essential to the war effort. However, with the loss of much of the population the community collapsed, and he moved the family to Albuquerque, then to Santa Fe where he worked as a laborer in construction.

Dad surprised us one day when he informed Mom he had found a new job, but was puzzled about the process of employment as he had to go to some office located at 109 East Palace Place near the Plaza.

We were greeted by a cheerful lady, Dorothy McKibben, who was in charge of employment for some super hush project up in the Jemez mountains about 35 miles north of Santa Fe in a place by the name of Los Alamos. To me I could have cared less where the job was as escaping from that apartment, kindergarten and all the negative memories of that environment was all the reason to be happy in relocating.

Everyone working in Los Alamos knew Dorothy McKibbin who became the den mother of every employee in Los Alamos. Ms. McKibbin was the primary liaison between the super hush program and the front office of the Project located in Santa Fe. All selected men and women to work on the Project had to pass through her office with no one having any idea what work they would be performing, who they would be working for, or where and how they would live. Difficult as it seemed, Ms. McKibbin managed to address all the logistics to keep supplies en route to Los Alamos, and support her boss, J. Robert Oppenheimer. On top of this were the daily rigid requirements for 24/7 security, especially the scientists who came from abroad. Ms. McKibbin spoke about Klaus Fuchs, the convicted spy who passed crucial secrets about the special project to the Russians, and still considered him to be a nice and gentle man.

My father's employer was Zia Company. The Zia Company was incorporated in the State of New Mexico for the primary purpose of balancing families and homes along with the support needed for the laboratory. Zia had a significant role in Los Alamos and the laboratory as it managed all the property, transportation, the Lodge,

Atomic Energy Commission, Hospital, Youth Center, School, library, cafeterias, fire department, radio station, newspaper and cold storage plant.

March 1943 the secret project in Los Alamos, New Mexico; The Manhattan Project, officially began. On August 15, 1943 the Chávez family, Dad, Mom, Dolores, two-week-old Lenora and I packed and loaded Dad's 1939 Chevy coupe with just our clothes, as we had no furniture, and headed to our new residence in Los Alamos. What was most intriguing to me was that this home would be furnished with standard and simple military furnishings, and with indoor plumbing, heating and electricity. I thought Dad had won the lottery.

Before beginning the ascent onto the mesas surrounding Los Alamos there was a fresh water well where the road presently forks to Española and continues to Santa Fe. We stopped there and had the most refreshing drink of water I have ever had from this artesian well, and filled the radiator in preparation for the steep climb ahead.

When we reached the top of the initial mountain plateau we were met with numerous U.S. Army Military Police surrounding all the vehicles entering Los alamos at what was known as West Gate where we were directed to stop. The primary guard gate was a small white wooden building into which we were escorted and Dad produced numerous sheets of paper for the Military Police.

Questions were asked of which I did not understand a word. Dolores and I tightly held onto each other as Mom took care of Lenora. We were finally asked to stand behind a camera and had our pictures taken, and Dad again had to read and fill out more papers. I still marvel how my father learned his limited English so quickly.

There are numerous books, research documents, and journals written about the development of the Atomic Bomb in Los Alamos.What follows is my own personal experience during my childhood in Los Alamos, and my life thereafter.

The home we were assigned was a small log cabin that originally belonged to the Boys Ranch, along with 52 other cabins that had been built to support the Boys Ranch. This was an exclusive school for the rich and famous at that time, but the government bought it to bring together the greatest minds in the field of physics, mathematics, chemistry, and numerous other scientific fields from all around the world to concentrate on the development of a super weapon to bring an end to World War Il. However, at the time we didn't know.

Our home was on the corner of two dirt roads next to the wooden water tower that originally provided water to the boy's ranch. The log cabin was small and simple as Abe Lincoln's, minus the oil burning lamps. It was a two-room cabin. One room was the kitchen, a small cramped dining area, a small gas stove, with a food pantry on one side near the rear door entry, and at the other end storage and closet room.

In the middle was our prized bathroom that had a shower and sink with hot and cold running water, and a toilet just like the one in the Mountainair restaurant. Mom also had a sink in the kitchen with hot and cold water, and the second room was a small area that during the day served as our living room, and in the evening our bedroom which was where the primary entry door was located to our small humble home. The address was a simple military control number that began with a large black letter T.

School was a much-awaited event as I was still not in command of the English language and I did not want to experience another event like the one in kindergarten in Santa Fe. (*Unable to ask using his limited English if he could use the bathroom, an accident occurred.*) The first constructed school in Los Alamos was built in 1943. It was located about a five-minute walk from our log cabin home and known as Central School, which had K-12 under one roof.

With only a short time to prepare myself for school the only assistance my parents could provide was courtesy. When a lady speaks to me, always say, "yes ma'm" or "no ma'm", and the same for a man, "yes sir, or no sir." This was not a very powerful vocabulary to face my teacher, and classmates. Central school had a total of eight classrooms for elementary and high school for a total enrollment of 140 students.

It is believed by leading educational experts that students' academic performance is primarily the quality of their teachers. That may be so if you are in a class where only one language is used, or well understood, but in my case I had a dual role to perform.

On my first day of school my father walked me to Central School and presented me to my first grade teacher, Ms. Ruth Quinlin, a lovely lady with a warm smile. Dad informed her that my English was not very good, but that I was most willing to learn as quickly as possible.

After all the students found a place to sit, our teacher introduced herself, and then handed out to all the students Our Daily Readers, and I began my indoctrination into the world of Dick, Jane, Spot the dog, and the famous Bouncing Red Ball. No sooner had we begun to read, I quickly found myself falling behind the class as I would read or hear the phrase in English, translate it into Spanish, and back to English and by then the rest of the class was pages ahead of me.

Ms. Quinlin was truly a blessing in my life as she immediately perceived the problem and difficulty I was having. She asked me to n remain after school and we discussed my difficulty, and this became a routine procedure for us as we would sit while she would coach me in the proper pronunciation of words, assist me in reading, and how to project myself with greater assurance. I shared this with my mother so she would know that I would be a little late getting home after school, and without my knowledge, my mother became secretly involved with my education.

My mother was the greatest cook, and never followed a recipe. The us most delicious aroma's poured out of her kitchen, which caught the s. attention of several women who used to walk by our home, many of whom happened to be the wives of some of the famous scientists living in Los Alamos.

One day when I arrived home after school I noticed some ladies talking with my mother in her kitchen, and taking notes as she spoke in if her limited English, as she discussed the cooking procedures for her different delicious Mexican dishes. After a few sessions, which my mother had with these ladies, mom instructed me to come home

198

immediately after school as she had a special surprise for me.

Upon arriving at home I would find one of the ladies I had seen before with my mother waiting for me to begin my special and private tutoring lessons in payment for my mother's assistance in teaching them how to prepare Mexican dishes. My tutors were wives of very famous scientists working in Los Alamos such as Mrs. Lois Bradbury, whose husband Norris Bradbury later became the second director of the Laboratory.

Mrs. Bradbury had three sons, James, John and David. John was in my class. There was also in mom's kitchen Mrs. Edward Teller, and Mrs. Ulam the wife of the famous physicist Stanislaw Ulam, all unknown lovely ladies to me at the time who went on to make a huge impression in my life. My mother, a beautiful lady from Torreon, accomplished all this for me with only a sixth-grade education.

A month later, July 15, 1945, I was playing at my friend's home, John Bradbury, whose father was a top research scientist at the Laboratory. John told me that something special was about to happen, and wanted to know if I could accompany him and his family up to Sawyer's Hill, which at the time served as both a picnic area and ski area. He said that it would require me to say nothing to my parents, only to get their permission to go with him and his family the morning of July 16 around 4:00 a.m.

I asked myself how in the world could a small eight year old boy living in the most secure and secret city in the world be granted permission by his parents to accompany the Bradbury family to this remote area at 4:00am in the morning on July 16,1945, and not tell them why? It sounded so ridiculous to me that I did not even bother to waste my time or listen to the uproar from my father after asking such a stupid question.

In the early morning on July 16, 1945 a very special event happened. The first atomic bomb, nicknamed "gadget" was detonated. John later informed me that it was an awesome sight to see even from 200 miles away. When I told Dad and Mom about this, they looked at me oddly and felt that I had probably eaten too much chili the4 night before.

Always looking for a way to make some money, I began to sell the Santa Fe New Mexican newspaper at TA-1, (Technical Area) which was the primary location for the Laboratory located not far from our home. To gain access into this restricted area one had th have a Top Secret Clearance and a special identification badge.

Around 5:00pm I would position myself just outside of the guard gate to sell my papers to all who were en route home. One person who always purchased a newspaper from me began to stand out from all of the rest. He was a tall thin gentleman who wore a pork pie hat and always had a pipe in his mouth and a gentle smile for me each day. What stood out most were his soothing ice blue eyes that seemed to dance as he looked at me when he smiled. I soon found out that this man was J. Robert Oppenheimer, the director of the laboratory known back then as Project "Y", or The Manhattan Project. By now he knew my name and I was drawn to this man like a magnet as there was a special charisma he possessed that commanded my attention.

I told my father about this man, and he knew the name well, but thought I was either mistaken, making it up, or overreacting because of the circumstances of Los Alamos. One day my comment about being Dr. Oppenheimer's paperboy was confirmed as my father and I were in the Trading Post picking up some items for my mother. My father was in line to pay when I heard a small crowd directly behind us talking to the man with the majestic blue eyes. As I turned towards the crowd Dr. Oppenheimer looked at me, smiled and said "Hello Dimas." My father noted the exchange and Dr. Oppenheimer's comment, and I proudly introduced my father to this famous man. As we walked home my father still could not believe that I knew The Man. Dr. Oppenheimer lived near our log cabin on the corner of Peach and 20th street in the area known as bathtub row.

It was during this time that I began to notice and experience something I used to hear my elders speak about in a hushed voice: racism against Mexicans. My mother had limited use of the English language and spoke with a pronounced accent. I would note that women would jump ahead of her in line at the butcher counter, or in line to check out. I also recall the butchers stating that they could not understand my mother when she spoke because of her accent so they would help someone else. My Mother never lost her composure, nor complained as she kept that radiant smile on her face and practiced patience, which I always admired.

Norris Bradbury became the second director of the laboratory in October 1945. So while Oppenheimer is the founder or father of Los Alamos, Norris Bradbury is its savior. Many families left Los Alamos, while others stayed and additional families arrived.

Los Alamos continued its growth and what was remarkable about this unique little town was that it had no elderly residents since the average age at that time was roughly less than forty. We had no undertaker or cemetery, and the residents paid no municipal taxes or owned no real property since everything belonged to the government. There was zero unemployment because, if anyone quit or lost his job, they had to leave and someone else would come to occupy their home.

Los Alamos, when it became an incorporated county in New Mexico, was the thirty-second county in the state, was designated on license plates with the number 32, and followed by the license plate number. Santa Fe County was #1, Bernalillo County was #2, Rio Arriba was #17, Taos was number #5, and Dona Ana County was #7. I used to know all 32, but that system is no longer in use. I recall how jealous many nearby counties were of Los Alamos since it was a government run and operated city. Many who drove to Española, Santa Fe or other locations from Los Alamos had their vehicles vandalized with the identity of the license plate. Many would go to Española or Santa Fe to have their plates issued so as not to display they were from Los Alamos.

In 1947 the government approved and built 352 Western Area Original Houses, and 251 Denver Steel Units. Shortly after their completion Dad was informed that we had to vacate our log cabin, along with several others in the neighborhood as they were going to be taken down to make room for other buildings. Our family was assigned to a new Denver Steel Unit located at 3886 Ridgeway Drive, and the anticipated part of this move was the two full size bedrooms, a bonanza for our family.

However, again the scent of racial discrimination crept in as homes made available by ZIA and the Laboratory was done on a point system, which meant that the higher your income, the higher the points for housing you were entitled to regardless of the size of your family. Mexican-American families whose working parent(s) were in the lower scale of income, had the highest ethnic representation in those homes, and we soon began to hear racial comments about the Denver Steel area referred to as Tortilla Flats.

Up to now Los Alamos had been a government owned community as no one was allowed to own a home. On the positive side, all maintenance was free. The Zia Company performed all electrical and plumbing issues and painted our home periodically. Mom once again became famous for her culinary ability and just being a sweet and wonderful lady. She became a legend with all Zia workers doing maintenance work at our home as she always fed them, provided fresh coffee, and cake. Whenever our home came up for maintenance work, there was a battle among the men as to which team would service our home knowing they would be treated well by my mother.

Grade school, middle school and high school were always a challenge for me based on my inability to speak and read English properly; how much harder I had to work and study than the others in my class. In addition to these obstacles, I was also up against the "A" team of classmates who were children of eminent scientific families that set the bar pretty high in achieving good grades. I used to share my frustrations with my mother, as she was always so easy and comforting to speak with regarding my feelings. Dad, from the old school, was rough and tough and did not stand for any nonsense, as the true meaning of life to him was hard work and doing a good job.

On My Own *is a simple straightforward tale of one man's life, leading him from the earliest days of the Manhattan Project, Central School where he learned to speak English, Los Alamos High School where he was '55 Class Favorite and to his surprise, Pep Club Sweetheart, to hard work and high jinks at Eastern New Mexico University for an education he earned himself, and then to employment at the Los Alamos Scientific Laboratory where, as Employee Relations Manager and inspired by his Down's Syndrome sister, he initiated a hiring program for the mentally or physically challenged. But this was just the beginning.*

He soon moved on to enter Government Service, working with the Executive Office of the President in the Office of Economic Opportunity and the Department of Health, Education and Welfare, followed by a stint with the National Science Foundation. In each case his reputation brought him to the attention of those who sought him out and he advanced steadily. Eventually the Central Intelligence Agency recruited him and with it spent his final career years traveling extensively around the world on a variety of assignments.

109 EAST   PALACE

Dorothy McKibbin

109 East Palace was the Los Alamos Santa Fe office which served as a reception desk, information center, and travel bureau. Scientists arrived there breathless, sleepless, and haggard, tired from riding on trains that were slow and trains that were crowded, tired from missing connections and having nothing to eat, or tired from waiting out the dawn hours in a railroad station. Often the traveler arrived days after he had been expected and settled down with a sigh into a chair at 109 East Palace as if he could never move again. One could almost see his fatigue dropping off and piling up against the old adobe walls.

Most of the new arrivals were tense with expectancy and curiosity. They had left physics, chemistry, and metallurgical laboratories, had sold their homes or rented them, had deceived their friends, and then had launched forth into an unpredictable world. They walked into the thick-walled quietness of the old Spanish dwelling at 109 East Palace expecting anything and everything, the best and the worst.

The scientists often arrived in a frantic hurry. One dashed in hatless and breathless after a hectic rush from Johns Hopkins University and panted in dismay, 'What, no ride up for an hour and a half? Why, I cut short a seminar in order to get here now!"

"Up" meant, to the Project members, those thirty-five miles to the site at Los Alamos. The site was universally called "the Hill" in Santa Fe. Sometimes we called it upstairs, but the Hill really stuck. The elevation of the Project was practically the same as that of Santa Fe, but the road between them dropped down into Tesuque, past Cuyamungue, and into the Nambe and Rio Grande valleys before it climbed the last steep ten miles to regain the lost altitude. The site rested on the flat mesas extending eastward from the Jemez Range.

"Up" meant, to the Project members, those thirty-five miles to the site at Los Alamos. . . . The elevation of the Project was practically the same as that of Santa Fe, but the road between them dropped down into Tesuque, past Cuyamungue, and into the Nambe and Rio Grande valleys before it climbed the last steep ten miles to regain the lost altitude. (Los Alamos Historical Museum)

Before going up, the atomic scientist was welcomed within the old walls of 109 East Palace, the oldest building east of the Governor's Palace in that part of Santa Fe. True, the calcimine on the walls was new, so new that it came off onto his coat if he leaned against it. The furniture was government issue. But the scientist hesitated among those old walls only long enough to get a pass to take him past the ancient cliff dwelling ruins and on to the plateau and its incredible laboratories.

A yellow map was inscribed for the new arrival, with red pencil marking every mile and every turn of his route up. He proceeded in his own car, in a staff car, or in one of the gargantuan Army buses parked outside, waiting to hurl their exhaust blasts 'In a rolling staccato at the shaky old *portal.*

The road winds near the pueblos of Santa Clara and San and after it leaves the valley of the Rio Grande it begins to climb. Large lava beds are visible, and black escarpments. Then, salmon-colored cliffs, clean and high, tower to the sky. The trees are taller, and the earth smells of pine needles. Leaving the black lava on one side, the road runs under tent-rock formations and cuts through a white pumice bed. The Jemez Range is of volcanic formation, so the tuff is soft and easy to cut. Many ruins of ancient cliff dwellings lie near the road,

Tsankawi, Tsirege, Frijoles, Puye, and many more as yet unnamed. The ruins of Otowi appear last as the road mounts to the top and runs past the guardhouse and on up to the scientific laboratories. The town is humming with rush and hurry, and military cars swarm all over its winding roads. Buildings have been erected overnight, and they look it.

When the Tech Area administrative staff arrived in March 1943, they stayed in Santa Fe until the buildings on the Hill were finished. They took over five offices at 109 East Palace and functioned there full blast until the end of April. Army guards crept around these offices and stood in the shadow of the *portales* day and night. The Director's office and the offices of the Business Manager, Procurement and Personnel were hives of activity. Telephones rang constantly, and since few lines were connected interoffice, secretaries chased from office to office to drag the person being called to the waiting telephone.

Since the housing, as well as the offices, on the Hill had not been completed, the Project rented four ranches within twenty miles of Santa Fe, and as the eager scientists arrived, they were assigned with their families to the ranches. The laboratories at the site were in a sketchy state, but that did not deter the workers. In the morning, buses (which could be station wagons, sedans, or trucks) left 109 to pick up the men at the ranches and take them to the Hill. Occasionally a driver forgot to stop at a ranch, and the stranded and frustrated scientist would call in a white heat. Because there was no way to get food up there for their lunches, we had box lunches prepared in Santa Fe and taken up for the noon hour. The restaurants must have thought there was a tremendous amount of picnicking going on somewhere.

In June, staff members were moved from the ranches and housed either on the Hill or at Frijoles Lodge. The Lodge, an isolated mountain inn situated in the Bandelier National Monument in the Jemez Range, was taken over by the Project because it was closer than the ranches and the workers could commute to the 'Hill more easily and less conspicuously. *Los Ritos de los Frijoles* is the site of old cliff dwellings and pueblo ruins, and the kivas and ceremonial cave had many an interested visitor that summer. By the end of summer, the apartments and dormitories were completed and all members of the technical staff were housed on the Hill.

Meanwhile, by the end of April all the offices at 109 except mine had been picked up and moved to the Hill. A variety of functions remained in Santa Fe: the buses departed from here and therefore 109 became a center for the shoppers from the Hill; it was and still is an information center, not too accurate, but always willing, for inquiries on how and here to get items ranging from horses to hair ribbons. Babies were parked here. Dogs were tied outside. Our trucks delivered baggage, press, and freight to the Hill, and even special orders of flowers, baby cribs, and pumpernickel.

Of all the incoming personnel, the Wacs and some of the soldiers were at their lowest ebb in this office. They had not been told what was going to happen to them. They had been alerted for overseas duty, but the overseas silence had been flung around the shoulders of their families. They were ectoplasm for about five days without even an PO number. One Wac told me she was not allowed to mention to her closest buddy the fact that she was going overseas and was whisked off of her cot at two A.M. to be sent silently on her way. When the train ran west and stopped at Lamy, she thought it was all a big mistake, The sand and pinion trees did not look like any ocean she had ever seen. The nightmare continued when she walked into an old mud building which had nothing marine about it and was told that she had thirty-five miles farther to go into "that beat-up land. " Many Wacs were tearful in those early days. They were good soldiers, but the shock was too much for them. Quite a few have I ushered gently into Army cars or buses and sent on their way weeping. Soldiers also had no other orders than Santa Fe, and they too were confused and apprehensive.

Tired families with small babies came in and said hopefully that they had sent their furniture to 109, but it didn't look like much of a home.. .

Thirty-five miles to go,' we told them.

Machinists dashed in and asked, "Where is the dance hall?" Thirty-five miles to go.

Well, I think I will leave my suitcase down here. I may not like it.

For security reasons, there was never any discussion of the work going on up there, needless to say. I could see that the new arrivals coming into the office for the first time were busting with curiosity and anticipation. Words were never spoken but the atmosphere was full of suppressed excitement. It was interesting to see how much the different types of employees knew about where they were going and what it was like when they first arrived. Many came in the greatest ignorance and were correspondingly astonished and confused.

For security reasons, also, the word "physicist" was taboo. If there was no stranger around and I was feeling very wicked, I would glance in all directions, examine the empty air, raise an eyebrow, and whisper tensely, blowing through my teeth like a suppressed wind instrument, "Are you a phhh ht?"

Some of the most famous physicists traveled under assumed names. We never spoke of anyone by the term Doctor or Professor, but always called him Mister. We never mentioned the names of Project people to anyone except Project members.

One day Dr. Enrico Fermi and Dr. Sam Allison were in the office waiting for a car to take them to the Hill. As I made out their passes, I tossed my head and informed them that we had to demote them down here and speak of them and to them as plain Mister. They strolled around the town while waiting. Near the Cathedral, they noticed a statue in the yard.

"Who is that?" asked Allison of Fermi.

"That is Archbishop Lamy," said Fermi.

"Shhhh, ' whispered Allison, grabbing Fermi's arm and glancing around cautiously. "Mrs. McKibbin would suggest we call him Mr. Lamy."

One bright afternoon I had a call from the Hill asking me if I saw anything in the sky that might be a Japanese balloon. The object was situated so many degrees from the sun, etc., and they had been 0b serving it from the site and would like to know how it appeared from Santa Fe. I bustled out and scanned the skies from the Plaza and then drove to the top of old Fort Marcy and looked and looked. Apprehension and fear crept around my mind and heart as I contemplated such a possibility, with full knowledge of the danger to the

Project. I could not see the object in question, but I did see little puffs of cloud, very frail and tenuous, which formed and reformed like vapor. Each one I imagined to be a small parachute with a missile attached.

I later discovered that a few Japanese balloons had been dropped in the Southwest putting the staff on the Hill, from the Director down, into a dither that day. While the Army sent up search planes, the scientists spent the afternoon craning their necks and evolving fantastic theories about the phenomenon. The Personnel Director, an astronomer by profession, was called upon in his dual capacity to settle the argument in order to get the staff back to work. Since even he would not make a flat statement, speculation continued until the next day. Again at noon, the same luminescent object appeared in the sky. Only then did the experts agree that it was nothing more nor less than the planet Venus, rarely seen in broad daylight.

Santa Feans soon became accustomed to the queer ways of the scientists. They claimed they could spot these people from a great distance. Frequently, a clerk in a shop, prompted more by western hospitality than by curiosity, automatically inquired, "Where are you from?" The Answer was always a stammered "Box 1663," as the speaker faded into the background. Security allowed them to say no more. Santa Feans knew what Box 1663 meant and felt smug about it. They referred to the place as the submarine base, or the place where submarine windshield wipers were made. They knew that inquiries caused acute embarrassment, and often a perfectly natural question froze on their lips.

We had a little trouble with the city police who complained that our large buses stopped too long outside our door and blocked traffic. The street was narrow and cars were allowed to park on only one side. Of course, we were on the other side. A bus could be a hazard when a large truck went screeching through the streets, particularly if a car was parked across the street from the bus. The buses were therefore allowed to stand only a short time in order to avoid these crises. Sometimes, the buses were too few or too late for the waiting mobs, I would be awakened at home in the middle of the night by a telephone call asking, Where is the bus?" As if I knew. . . !

As most of the business between 109 and the Hill was transacted by telephone, the shortage of lines caused us great difficulty. A scientist rushing into the office in a great hurry before boarding a train would tear his hair while the operator told us endlessly, "line is busy." In the early days, the record time in getting a call through was an hour and a half and the delay was particularly rugged when someone was waiting on long distance for us to make the contact for him. Now there ?many lines, and we no longer have difficulty in getting our numbers.

All kinds, ages and and conditions of people came to 109 seeking employment on the Hill. The personnel work was fascinating. We did some initial interviewing, and if people seemed qualified, they were given extensive applications to fill out. One officer who had been overseas with several different combat units listed his occupation as "murder." A woman who had worked in one of the mess halls listed her "equipment used" as "blue uniform and hair nets."

To work on the Project, new employees had to be cleared by Security. Waiting for clearance was difficult for many people, and we had to go through their agonies with them. The two weeks required to check on them often consumed their funds and their spirits. They were tossed out of hotels every three days, and the scarcity of housing in this Land of Enchantment made the waiting doubly difficult.

Observing a place grow from one hundred to thousands of families is extremely absorbing. I was on excellent terms with many of the scientists and was more aware of their affairs than were most of the people in Santa Fe. There were weddings, divorces, and always many, many births. There was the constant arriving and departing from 109 East Palace. The first year of the Project's existence was celebrated with due ceremony, and then the second. We have now celebrated our third year. Babies who once slept in the office in their bassinets while their mothers shopped are now rushing around my desk and tearing the Scotch tape out of its holder.

When we were employed we were told to ask no questions, and we didn't—much. We worked with pride. We sensed the excitement and suspense of the Project, for the intensity of the people coming through the office was contagious. Working at 109 was more than just a job. It was an exciting experience. Our office served as the entrance to one of the most significant undertakings of the war, or indeed, of the twentieth century.

Standing By and Making Do: Women of Wartime Los

Alamos Paperback – September 22, 2008
by Jane S. Wilson (Editor), Charlotte Serber (Editor)

Acknowledgments

From Ellen

Ann Dilworth, my friend editor and advisor.
Jim and Carolyn Montman for their help with research and photos.
Sylvie Baumgartner, investigator of the long aftermath of nuclear research.
Molly Mayfield masking many valuable suggestions for improvement to the manuscript.
Diane Dunne, for reading the manuscript.
David Shiang for his helpful advice.
Katy Bradbury Lormand for support and love.
John Wymond Bradbury for his invaluable untangling of my computer.
Kim Pips, for her friendship.
Julie Fisher Melton, for sharing our stories.
David Wargo for his great and generous support.
Marie Bass, for listening to me.
Maggie Fine, who has listened to parts of the story.
Jim Bradbury for helping me think about this.
Margit Pearson, for her friendship and advice.
Cheryl Rolfer, for her knowledge and advice.
Linda Deck, Director the Bradbury Museum at Los
    Alamos.
Jim Walton, former Director of the National Museum
    of Atomic History.

215

Sandra Blakeslee, for friendship and help, and
especially for her amazing editorial work on the
manuscript.

Jill Cooper Udahl, Linda Durman, Romona Schoulder,
for friendship.

Bill Lanouette, For his advice.

Todd Nicklos, Director Los Alamos Historical Society.

Lauren Reid Anderson, for support and love.

John Coster-Mullen, what a guy!

Gregg Herken, exploring the Manhattan Project.

Cheryl Rolfer, information and friendship.

Stanley Goldberg, whose enthusiasm never wavered.

Mimi Roberts for great advice.

Michael Motley for a great cover design.

Studio X for great computer support.

From Marshall

Our first editor: Michael Wilt for his great help and
numerous improvements to the manuscript

Gale Wilder – my wife for her patience, numerous
reads of the manuscript, corrections and suggestions
for improvement.

Thanks to Michael Motley for the cover design.

John East for his reading, suggestions and corrections.

John Bourgoin for his reading and encouragement.

My previous editor, Lynn Elsey from my previous
book, *The Microchip Revolution* for her helpful and
insightful questions.

Annie Shabanow for her constant encouragement and
support.

Authors' biographies

Ellen graduated from the University of New Mexico in
1963 with a degree in Art History. Ellen went on to a
successful career as Director and Curator of Art at several
museums, including The Minneapolis Institute of Art and

the New Mexico Museum of Fine Arts in Santa Fe. She co-wrote and published a successful book *From the Far Away Nearby* on Georgia O'Keeffe. This book was published by the UNM Press in 1992. She also has written or co-written books on Mexican Architecture, and the American Indian Ghost Dance. More recently she founded and managed Recursos de Santa Fe, with a strong focus on the history of the US Southwest and the history of Los Alamos and the development of the atomic bomb. Ellen lives in Santa Fe, NM.

Marshall graduated from the University of New Mexico in 1964 with a BSEE in Electrical Engineering. After UNM Marshall moved to California where he earned a MSEE from Santa Clara, CA, and had a successful career in the Silicon Valley semiconductor industry. He started working at Fairchild Semiconductor in 1965 when the industry was very new, and worked for 8 different companies, including Advanced Micro Devices and Synergy Semiconductor, which he co-founded. His last industry position was as a senior manager at Broadcom. After retiring, he co-wrote a book on the early history of the semiconductor industry. It is titled *The Microchip Revolution*, published on Amazon in 2020. Marshall lives with his wife, Gale in San Jose, CA

Made in the USA
Middletown, DE
05 November 2023

41861108R00129